Documents in Contemporary History

General editor

Kevin Jefferys

Faculty of Arts and Education, University of Plymouth

DERBY COLLEGE · WILMORTON PLA

Television and the press since 1945

MANCHESTER
UNIVERSITY PRESS

Documents in Contemporary History is a series designed for sixth-formers and undergraduates in higher education. It aims to provide both an overview of specialist research on topics in post-1939 British history, and a wide-ranging selection of primary source material.

Already published in the series

Forthcoming

Documents in Contemporary History

Television and the press since 1945

Edited by

Ralph Negrine

Senior Lecturer in Mass Communications, Centre for
Mass Communication Research, University of Leicester

Manchester University Press
Manchester and New York

Distributed exclusively in the USA by St. Martin's Press

Copyright © Ralph Negrine 1998

The right of Ralph Negrine to be identified as the author of this work has been asserted by him in accordance with the Copyright, Designs and Patents Act 1988.

Published by Manchester University Press
Oxford Road, Manchester M13 9NR, UK
and Room 400, 175 Fifth Avenue, New York, NY 10010, USA
http://www.man.ac.uk/mup

Distributed exclusively in the USA by
St. Martin's Press, Inc., 175 Fifth Avenue, New York, NY 10010, USA

Distributed exclusively in Canada by
UBC Press, University of British Columbia, 6344 Memorial Road, Vancouver, BC, Canada V6T 1Z2

British Library Cataloguing-in-Publication Data
A catalogue record for this book is available from the British Library

Library of Congress Cataloging-in-Publication Data applied for

ISBN   0 7190 4920 2   *hardback*
       0 7190 4921 0   *paperback*

First published 1998

05 04 03 02 01 00 99 98   10 9 8 7 6 5 4 3 2 1

Printed in Great Britain
by Bell & Bain Ltd, Glasgow

Contents

Acknowledgements

The publisher and editor would like to thank the following for granting permission to reproduce copyright material:

Angus and Robertson (5.7)
Associated Business Press (4.15)
Association of British Editors (5.21)
Aurum Press and Lord W. Whitelaw (1.15)
Cabinet Office (5.26)
Coronet (5.6 and 4.20)
Economist Intelligence Unit (4.9)
Faber and Faber (2.13)
Greater London Council and Sheffield City Council (2.14)
The Guardian (1.22, 2.21, 5.19, 5.22, 5.24 and 5.25)
Hansard Society and William Kimber (3.19)
HarperCollins (1.12)
Heinemann (5.5)
Her Majesty's Stationery Office (HMSO)
Hutchinson (1.8)
I. B. Taurus (3.27)
Independent Television Commission (1.21, 1.24, 2.19, 3.14 and 3.15)
John Libbey (1.18)
Labour Party (2.25)
Macmillan (3.12 and 4.14)
Methuen / Routledge and International Thomson Publishing Services
    Limited (4.21)
Mr Hugo Young and the Scott Trust (5.8)
Mr R. Bolton (3.33)
New Statesman (5.10)
Pluto Press (4.16)

Acknowledgements

Political Quarterly (1.16)

Professor Jeremy Tunstall and Peters Fraser and Dunlop Group Ltd (5.23)

Rogers, Coleridge and White (4.17)

Scan Books (5.4)

Secker & Warburg (1.3)

Sidgwick & Jackson and Macmillan (3.30 and 3.31)

The Bodley Head (3.9, 5.2, 3.7 and 3.29)

The Rt. Hon. Jack Straw, MP (3.25)

Weidenfield & Nicholson and Mr Robin Day (3.20 and 3.21)

Whilst every effort has been made to contact the appropriate publishers, it has not been possible to trace the ownership of some copyrighted material. Any person claiming copyright should contact the publisher.

Chronology

1969	*Aide Mémoire* revised.
1969	Rupert Murdoch acquires *The Sun*.
1971	*Daily Sketch* merges with the *Daily Mail*.
1972	Community television experiments start.
1977	*Report of the Committee on the Future of Broadcasting* (Annan report) published.
1977	Royal Commission on the Press 1974–77 report published.
1981	Report of a Home Office Study, *Direct Broadcasting By Satellite* published.
1982	Channel 4 launched.
1982	Information Technology Advisory Panel, *Cable Systems* report published.
1982	*Mail on Sunday* launched.
1982	Sky Channel, a satellite service, begins broadcasting across Europe.
1983	First cable systems licences awarded.
1983	Home Office and Department of Industry, *The Development of Cable Systems and Services* report published.
1984	*Television Without Frontiers* document released by European Commission.
1985	*Real Lives: At the Edge of the Union* BBC programme held up. One-day strike of journalists in broadcasting.
1986	Direct Broadcasting by Satellite (DBS) contract awarded to British Satellite Broadcasting (BSB), a consortium of mainly British media groups.
1986	*The Independent* newspaper launched.
1986	News International moves to Wapping.
1986	*Report of the Committee on Financing the BBC* (Peacock report) published.
1986	*Today* newspaper launched.
1988	Broadcasting Ban introduced.
1988	*Broadcasting in the '90s: Competition, Choice and Quality* White Paper published.
1989	British Satellite Broadcasting (BSB) launched.
1989	European Union Directive on cross-frontier television published.
1989	Sky Television launches on the Astra satellite.
1989	Television cameras enter the House of Commons.
1990	Broadcasting Act published.

1990	Sky Television and BSB merge to form BSkyB, with Murdoch having a majority stake.
1991	ITV franchises awarded for ten years.
1992	Government changes rules of ITV company ownership.
1994	Broadcasting Ban removed.
1995	*Today* shut down by News International.
1996	Broadcasting Act published.
1997	Channel 5 launched.

Introduction

Since 1945, the mass media in Britain – and Britain itself – have changed considerably. Writing about that change is, at the best of times, a difficult task; attempting to write about it through historical documents is even more so: what documents does one select, and what counts as a historical document for our purposes? Other problems soon emerge: is it best to organise the material around certain key themes such as 'the freedom of the press', or should the material be focused on different media thus differentiating between the press and television or television and the 'new' media? Should it be about processes in communication or about media structures? (See Dahl, 1994.) Given the problematic nature of these questions, it may be useful at this point to set out how this volume was conceived and how the material has been organised.

Media history

In the immediate post-war period, radio was still the dominant means of mass communication in Britain. Television was still very much in its infancy and the press was adjusting to a period of newsprint rationing. By the end of the period under review, the press was still an important means of communication but it was television that had become *the* mass medium, and part of a multi-media environment which included video recorders, computers, faxes and the internet.

All these changes are fairly easy to describe but they point to a fundamentally different set of relationships between the listener/viewer/consumer in the late 1940s and the listener/viewer/consumer in the late 1990s: where once there was a BBC monopoly in sound and vision, there is now a plethora of choice in sound and vision. In

1

sheer numbers – of radio or television services – the picture in the 1990s is thus very different from the picture in the 1940s. To take one simple and illustrative example, in the mid-1950s commercial television was born and this doubled the number of terrestrial television channels available in Britain; in the 1990s the average cable viewer has access to over thirty television services.

The actual increase in numbers masks two important factors that also need to be taken into account if some sense is to be made of the changes. One of these factors is that despite the numerical increase in services, some services (BBC, ITV) continue to dominate viewing in most households. The other factor is that although these dominant broadcasters have adapted to the new communications environment, they have not abandoned the public service principles of broadcasting.

The organisation of the material in this volume attempts to emphasise both the *continuities* and the *discontinuities* that can be identified in the development of the mass media over the last fifty years. Inevitably, the selection of material to illustrate points will provide a narrative of sorts, and in doing so it will provide an overview of the historical development of the mass media in Britain. Sometimes the selections will focus on specific themes, e.g. 'the press and privacy', but at other times the emphasis will be on media, e.g. cable television. The decision of which of the two approaches to use was partly dictated by whether or not it was simpler to document things by medium rather than by theme. Often, the two approaches overlap. One cannot, for example, discuss the technological change in the newspaper industry without, at the same time, confronting the long tradition of antipathy to government interference, i.e. 'threats' to the 'freedom of the press'.

The five chapters thus provide the means by which one can organise the material into significant narratives on the development of the major mass media in Britain since 1945.

Which media? Which documents?

The collection of extracts in this volume attempts to illustrate patterns of continuity and change with respect to specific media. The press and the broadcast media, including cable and satellite television, feature most prominently. There are, inevitably, some important omissions: there is nothing on the medium of radio, on the development and use of video recorders, on the internet and digital technology, on the increasingly European dimension of television broadcasting, on the interface between domestic and international forces. Part of the reason for not including much on newer technologies is that it is too early to say how they will fit into the multi-media environment of the twenty-first century.

Narrowing the focus of the volume does not, however, make it any easier to select extracts from relevant documents. The choice of documents, *any choice of documents*, takes the reader along a particular path (and away from another). The same applies to the specific extracts that are selected from the documents. Are they representative? Do they accurately portray the arguments?

What, then, has informed the present selection? The first consideration was to choose extracts from primary documents rather than secondary analysis of the material. Such documents would be 'original' in some way and so reflect the context in which they were produced. Into this category would fall all the documents of the Royal Commissions on the Press and the Committees on Broadcasting, and publications from particular departments, such as the Department of National Heritage on media ownership, or commissioned from named individuals by ministers, such as David Calcutt's report on 'privacy, self-regulation and the press'.

Whilst it is clearly impossible *not* to include extracts from these documents, it is important to bear in mind that their 'official' status is no indication whatsoever of their actual *significance* in terms of initiating or directing developments. There is a 'politics of inquiries' which cannot be ignored and which often leads to a quite different interpretation of the outcome of the inquiries themselves and of the worth of the final report.

Lord Beaverbrook, for instance, felt that aim of the 1947–49 Royal Commission on the Press was 'without doubt to persecute the press' (Taylor, 1974: 747). Lord Annan's Committee on the Future of Broadcasting (1977) fared no better:

> Within ITV Lord Annan was seen as a good choice for chairman: a worldly academic, politically middle-of-the-road. But the rest of the names inspired no confidence that the report would be fair and balanced. Not a single one of the sixteen members was identifiable as what might be described as an ITV viewer and, to judge an industry with a multimillion pound

turnover, fifteen out of the sixteen had no first-hand experience of business. Leading campaigners against advertising and the whole ITV system were included. (Potter, 1989: 225)

Similar comments could be made of the 1985 Peacock Committee on Financing the BBC, which was commonly regarded as an attempt to 'get at' the BBC.

The membership of committees, the competence of the committee members, and the agendas – implicit or explicit – which committees take on have therefore a great bearing on how the work of these committees will be viewed by others. Jeremy Tunstall, for instance, has criticised the 1961–62 Royal Commission on the Press for failing to consider the 'profound consequences for the press of the emergence of television' (1980: 125), and he has criticised the 1974–77 Royal Commission on the Press and the Annan Committee on the Future of Broadcasting for not engaging more fully in a dialogue on the rapidly changing nature of the media in the late 1970s. One other reflection on the nature of committees is provided by Samuel Brittan who sat on the Peacock Committee (see 1.17).

The list of primary documents – criticisms notwithstanding – is nevertheless vast and they are a rich source of information. However, there are fewer such documents on the press than on the broadcast media in general. One reason for this is that the broadcast media are regulated whilst the press is not. Consequently, on each occasion that a decision is made with respect to broadcasting, the inquiry process produces many documents. By contrast, because the press is not regulated in the same way and is only touched by certain forms of government activity, e.g. with respect to monopolies and mergers, there is not the same process of investigation and report writing.

Other sources also feature in this volume. These include extracts from memoirs or personal accounts of events. Such extracts provide a view into the often 'private' dimension of policy-making or debate. They can thus add a different kind of information to primary documents. They can also reveal how the public consideration of events meshes with the private process of decision-making and debate. In so doing, they highlight the process of interaction which helps to account for media developments. This would be as true of Tony Benn's musings on the BBC (see 1.8) as of William Whitelaw's decisions about Channel 4 (see 1.15).

A final source of extracts is commentaries on events or media drawn from books or newspapers. These are not primary documents in the sense used above but their inclusion was dictated by the fact that they add to our understanding of the process of development or of debates. Furthermore, because the media are very public there are many individuals and authorities who comment on them and add to the debate. Channel 4, for instance, was created in a context in which individuals and authorities, in and out of the media, contributed to a long and complex discussion about the future of broadcasting in Britain. Those contributions became part of the debate itself and so deserve to be listed. It would, therefore, be a mistake not to include the full range of available material which throws light on historical and contemporary developments.

Each of the five chapters combines extracts from these sources of information to provide a fairly coherent account of some key developments in the mass media in Britain since 1945. The extracts have been chosen to reflect these developments, although it should be borne in mind that as each of the extracts comes from much larger documents the selection represents a very small part of a larger – and often extremely interesting – set of documents.

The organisation of this volume

The material has been arranged into five chapters. Three of these chapters deal with broadcasting: Chapter 1 focuses on developments in television, Chapter 2 on the 'new' media of cable and satellite, and Chapter 3 on aspects of political broadcasting. In view of the comments made by Jeremy Tunstall (above), it is worth noting that the latter parts of Chapters 1 and 2 begin to overlap as convergence between media becomes an issue in itself.

The remaining two chapters are on the press. Chapter 4 traces developments in the press since 1945, whilst Chapter 5 is a more loosely arranged chapter in which several different aspects of the press and its practices, e.g. the 'Lobby' system or issues of privacy, are highlighted.

The extracts follow the main themes of each chapter. Often they are placed in a chronological order. They are chosen from documents which are listed at the end of each extract. As the documents are usually long, the extracts are meant to represent the key themes within any specific chapter or analysis, or the basic elements of a particular argument.

Terrestrial television, 1945–1998

The rate of technological change since 1945 has been dramatic. Yet that change has presented both opportunities and problems in the field of communications: opportunities in that new arrangements and new forms of communication could be put in place, and problems in that old regulatory mechanisms have needed to be adapted to the new environment. One good illustration of this from the immediate post-war period is the debate about commercial television. Although the BBC controlled the air-waves in both radio and television broadcasting, it was clear that technical developments allowed for more services than actually existed. For many, then, technical change presented new opportunities in the field of broadcasting. But for governments, the possibilities of new services presented a whole series of problems: who would fund such services, who would control them, what should they be allowed to broadcast? Furthermore, could such change be made in a system which valued the principles of public service broadcasting? Could those principles be adapted to a commercial television system?

In the event, commercial television was incorporated into the broadcasting system and it was given public service responsibilities. Over time, the broadcasting structure has retained some important features: the licence fee remains a significant source of funding for the BBC and the divide between a licence-fee-funded BBC and a commercially funded television sector remains as strong today as it was in the mid-1950s. By accident rather than design, perhaps, the structure of broadcasting in Britain has remained strong and it continues to produce material of high quality as it adapts to new technological challenges and competition. One factor which has helped it retain its characteristics must surely be the process of regulation that is in place. Apart from regular reviews, both the public and commercial television sectors are overseen in some way or other: governors in the case of the BBC, the Independent Television Commission (previously IBA, and ITA) in the case of commercial television. Whilst the system has not been without its problems, it is one which provides some element of supervision of quality.

When seeking to track the origin of structural change in the post-war period – and it must be remembered that the story of change dates back to earlier times – one must inevitably start with the 1949 Broadcasting Committee. Although the decision to create commercial television came out of a more prolonged debate, this Committee provided a focus for discussions and saw the beginnings of a serious argument for change.

The introduction of commercial television and the content of this new service became an issue in itself when the next committee of inquiry into broadcasting was set up in 1960. By then, commercial television had been in existence for some five years and although some of its consequences had been favourable, e.g. with respect to the development of news and political broadcasting, many others were regarded as undesirable (see 1.6 and 1.7). Criticisms of commercial television, therefore, featured quite prominently in the 1960 Committee on Broadcasting report (see 1.6) and led to the BBC being granted the powers to run the third television service which became BBC2. In spite of the favourable treatment which the BBC obtained from the 1960 Committee, there was a certain amount of antipathy towards it from one prominent minister, Tony Benn, in the mid-1960s (see 1.8).

Changes in the social make-up of Britain gave rise to different views on the role of broadcasting within society. Whereas the 1960 Committee was content with a version of the 'purposes of broadcasting' perhaps suited to the mid-1950s, the next three decades provided very different contexts within which broadcasting could be analysed. The Annan Committee (1977) was concerned with the need to reflect the multitude of interests in Britain (see 1.9), whilst the Peacock Committee in the mid-1980s had to contend with a totally different media landscape where the viewer could be considered a consumer who could exercise a choice between services (see 1.16). It is interesting to contrast the 1960 Committee's views on broadcasting (see 1.6) with those of the Peacock Committee (1986) (see 1.16). The latter was less prepared to consider a single version of what is best in television, preferring to celebrate the diversity that could come about as a result of technological change and greater consumer choice. In these differences of perspective, was there still something which could be defined as 'public service broadcasting'?

The key event in the late 1970s must be the creation of Channel 4. Numerous proposals were put forward on the form the new service should take (see 1.12–15) before a final version emerged. But the essence of the service, as defined in the 1980s, began to change in the 1990s as it competed directly with ITV and began, according to some accounts, to lose sight of its original remit. In the view of many, it would have to re-define its remit in the context of a new, multi-media environment (see 1.24).

By the late 1980s, although the duopoly was still intact – despite the growth of both satellite and cable systems – many issues remained unresolved. Who should get the licence to run the fifth channel? How should independent television companies be regulated? How should one choose between one franchise applicant and another? How should Channel 4 be funded? What should Channel 4's relationship to the other television companies be?

Answers to some of these were found in the Peacock Committee report. Though the government of Margaret Thatcher did not accept the full implications of the report itself, many of its recommendations were in fact incorporated into the 1990 Broadcasting Act (see 1.20).

The 1990s also saw a growth of interest in how broadcasters should work on the international level. The attempt to create a more broadly based and more competitive media structure in the UK – the creation of large media groups, for example – required the re-writing of the ownership rules, amongst other things, and efforts to guess the future pattern of change. The problem was, though, that other media – such as cable and satellite – muddied the picture somewhat and that the advent of digital terrestrial and digital satellite television, with their promise of hundreds of channels, made any attempt at prediction an extremely difficult business.

In this catalogue of change, one thing was abundantly clear. Governments could no longer control broadcasting developments as they had done in the 1940s when there were so few players and when all those players were domestic ones. The international dimension of broadcasting – in ownership terms, in regulatory terms and in terms of content transfers – would mean that developments in the domestic arena were as much the product as the cause of changes taking place elsewhere.

The end of scarcity

The monopolistic control exercised by the BBC allowed it to do many things, including the development of a particular programming policy of 'the best of everything' which was often 'threatened' by the possibility of commercially run broadcasters.

One of the earliest perceived threats came from the radio relay services of the 1920s. Little came of this as the BBC, with help from the Post Office, was able to curtail their development and to contain the potential for change. In effect, the BBC sought to limit what the radio relay operators could do to its own vision of broadcasting by relaying or 'importing' more popular fare from the Continent, for example.

After 1945, similar issues were to come to the fore. At each stage, any attempt by non-BBC, and later non-ITV, broadcasters to break away from the existing pattern of broadcasting was rejected. In the late 1940s and early 1950s many private companies were willing to start offering new things on the existing relay systems, including via some form of subscription or pay-television, but these efforts were turned down for fear of upsetting the delicate broadcasting system then controlled by the BBC, and later by the duopoly (see 2.1–4). Often, the rejection was founded on the idea that commercial forms of broadcasting would damage what was best in the broadcasting system (see 2.4).

But, as documents show, others were less certain of the need to reject new forms of broadcasting out of hand. There was a willing-ness within some governmental circles to permit new developments. Some did develop in the 1960s in the form of the pay-television experiments (see 2.6). These experiments were still only that, experi-ments, and there was much less willingness to grant them the right to compete as equals with the members of the duopoly.

Some cable operators felt that they needed to show that they were not only interested in profit-making and that they wanted to provide, through their systems, community facilities in the form of community television. In this way, they could prove their worth to the community and justify their claims to being another set of legitimate broadcasters within the British broadcasting system. In 1972 the government licensed the community television experiments but they were restricted in what they could do: they could not, initially, show adver-tisements, for example.

At the same time as these changes were taking place, there were also inquiries into the changing technology of broadcasting. One of the key questions was whether cable systems had a future, and whether that future included the possibility of offering a national infrastructure for communication. From the late 1960s, the future of cable was becoming associated with the idea of the 'wired nation' and the potential for a connected society. Unfortunately, the costs of wir-ing the nation were too prohibitive and the technology not suffi-

ciently advanced to allow for what was being promised. Consequently, cable systems were sidelined (see 2.7 and 2.8).

Interest in cable systems was rekindled under the Thatcher government through the work of the Information Technology Advisory
Panel (ITAP). The Panel placed cable systems at the centre of a
national infrastructure: creating that infrastructure would permit
Britain to advance technologically and to benefit economically as well
(see 2.10 and 2.11). The ITAP proposed that cable systems should
develop in the private sector with a minimum amount of regulation
and that they should be able to use the demand for entertainment as a
way of building up the cable infrastructure. This was the 'entertain-
ment-led' philosophy.

Developments took longer than anticipated. Certain economic
policies damaged cable's progress (see 2.13), but cable systems were
also to suffer from a lack of high quality programming, high costs of
installing systems, and the coming of satellite television. Satellite
television, like cable, could provide many entertainment channels,
but at a fraction of the cost of cable systems: the technology was
cheaper to use, and prospective viewers would not have to wait to be
cabled before they could access these services. Installing a dish –
something which became progressively cheaper – would achieve
instant results (see 2.15–19).

Rupert Murdoch had a dramatic success with Sky Television –
both in terms of being able to buy rights to important sporting events,
and in terms of being able to beat his satellite television rival (see 2.20
and 2.21). BSkyB became *the* satellite broadcaster and in direct competition with cable television operators.

To add to the competitive environment, the telecommunications
provider British Telecom (BT) was also keen on entering the entertainment market. After privatisation, it was not permitted to do so
until well into the next century, but the new Labour government
decided in 1998 that BT should be permitted to provide entertainment by the year 2000 (see 2.22 and 2.23).

In the face of these competitive forces, the cable industry did not
fare too well, and its growth has been slow. A Parliamentary Office of
Science and Technology report showed immense concern over this
issue (see 2.24) at about the same time that the Labour Party under
Tony Blair began to look forward to a 'wired society', although in
that original vision it was BT which was to do much of the wiring (see
2.23–25).

Introduction

At the turn of the century the dominant players are the same as those in the 1990s: Rupert Murdoch and BSkyB, the cable companies, BT, with the terrestrial broadcasters continuing to be strong on the programming side of the industry. Digital television, terrestrial and satellite, will add to the menu available to viewers but the menu providers will be no different from those currently in place. One of the unresolved issues is who will control much of the technology which will grant access to the promised plethora of services: will it be Murdoch with, or without, allies? Will the regulators permit him to dominate the market?

Broadcasting and political communication

It is difficult to look back at the early years of broadcasting without puzzling over the extent to which the broadcasting organisations shied away from the coverage of politics. In the period up to the mid-1950s the broadcasters faced the political world with a lack of certainty as to how it should be covered. Part of the reasons for that lay in the belief amongst the broadcasters, then only the BBC, that Parliament was the place for political debate. If broadcasting intruded into that world, it would risk undermining Parliament and creating a different venue for politics. Such reasoning lay behind the 14-Day Rule which restricted what the broadcasters could report on. Its effect was to negate the notion that broadcasting could offer a public space for debate and discussion, even though it was becoming a medium of some importance (see 3.1–6). Though the Rule was itself restrictive, it should also be added that broadcasters – again, mainly the BBC – had no real sense of how to cover news and current affairs, as commonly understood today. The early 1950s thus marked the transition from radio to television and from newsreel to more modern forms of news (see 3.7).

The difficult relationship between the broadcasters and the world of politics can be seen in the section on the televising of the House of Commons. That the debate over this issue went on for so long shows very clearly the suspicions that politicians have of the broadcasters and of the broadcasters usurping their role and the role of Parliament. For many, Millbank – the centre for political television in London – has become an alternative Parliament.

The 14-Day Rule was undoubtedly unpopular amongst the broadcasters and it was eventually abandoned in 1956 (see 3.8). Some of the pressure for change came from different practices being developed for election coverage, the advent of the commercial news services and the Suez crisis (see 3.9, 3.27 and 3.29).

All of these things changed the face of political broadcasting. They created a new form of inquiry into politics and a new form of reporting of politics which permitted political actors to be interviewed in ways unknown at the beginning of the 1950s (see 3.20 and 3.21).

Three other things about this period are worth noting. The first is the *Aide Mémoire* which determined how broadcasts by ministers would be treated, the second is the Representation of the People Act which does not permit candidates for political office to buy air-time, and the third is the rules of political coverage and the distribution of time for party political broadcasting which were devised by the BBC and the political parties. In all three, one finds the creating of procedures for action. One of these, the *Aide Mémoire*, played a crucial role in the coverage of the Suez crisis (see 3.28).

The final section of Chapter 3, which covers the reporting of the Suez crisis and the troubles in Northern Ireland, illustrates the limits of political communication and the mechanisms of control which are used on the broadcasters when governments wish to keep things off the screen. One interesting link in these two sections are letters between members of government and the BBC seeking to restrict the coverage of instances. In the cases cited, the government minister in charge of broadcasting – the Postmaster General, then the Home Secretary, then the Minister for National Heritage, and now the Minister of Culture, Media and Sport – sought to retain the myth of the BBC as a neutral and impartial organisation, whilst also imposing controls over the organisation. The commercial companies are not immune either, as the study of the programme *Death on the Rock* shows (see 3.30–34).

The British press: an overview of the post-war period

Unlike broadcasting, there is no easy way of dividing up the period covered by this volume for the purpose of analysing the newspaper industry. There are clearly landmarks which one can take note of, but the period as a whole cannot be broken up easily into ready-made blocks for analysis. Often, the landmarks are only points worthy of comment, and the points of references simply ways of organising the material.

Moreover, one cannot find the regular drip of governmental papers (Acts, White Papers, etc.) which are characteristic of dealings in the broadcast media. But the absence of a continuous flow of primary documentation is perhaps more than made up by the plethora of other sources of information on the press which can be searched. These are plentiful and cover everything from analysis of content to biographies of editors. Most come from academic institutions, though many now come from journalists themselves. Nevertheless, the chapters here rely more heavily on primary documentation.

Both chapters on the press look at the broad organisation of the industry. They do not detail individual changes of ownership of titles or even changes of editors for the simple reason that there have been too many of these – particularly of the latter in the last decade – to comment on. It is the broad sweep of changes in the industry which is the focus of these two chapters. Yet in exploring the industry over this period, one finds some interesting points of comparison. The similarities between the late 1940s and the late 1990s include:

- an industry that is still privately owned (although the nature of that ownership may have changed);
- an industry that continues to be self-regulated (despite threats to introduce other mechanisms);
- an industry that does not get any state-aid;
- a relative stability with regards to the number of national newspapers published;
- a continuing concern about concentration of ownership and absence of diversity (though this too has become more muted of late).

The differences include:

- a changing media context with the development of a plethora of different and competing media;
- a shift away from traditional printing technologies and the introduction of different printing technologies and design styles;
- closer alliance between (some) newspapers and other media (this is part and parcel of the changing nature of ownership);
- a move away from Fleet Street;
- some significant changes in circulation for national newspapers.

Of these, it is perhaps the similarities that stand out: the industry continues to be self-regulated and it remains a highly competitive one. Both these factors help us to understand the continuing concerns about the possible death of titles and the lack of diversity *and* the reasons why schemes to help the industry never get beyond the drawing board. As Jeremy Tunstall has written, 'in the press, the traditional policy is of not having a policy' (1983: 122).

The extracts in Chapter 4 revolve around these factors. Included in this chapter is material from the three Royal Commissions (1947–49, 1961–62 and 1974–77) and other related documents on sets of topics:

- on the nature of the press, its performance and the 'problems' (e.g. inefficiency of production) of the industry (see 4.1–3, 4.5, 4.8, 4.10, 4.11. 4.14–17);
- on concentration of ownership (see 4.12);
- on possible schemes to help the industry (see 4.7, 4.13, 4.18–20);
- on the view that the industry could be helped by more efficient production and the introduction of computerised technology (see 4.9 and 4.21);
- on contemporary changes in newspapers (see 4.21 and 4.22).

But these extracts need to be seen within the context outlined above, as well as some of the main interpretations of the issues and problems within the industry in this period. Underlying all these concerns is a simple idea or, perhaps more accurately, a collection of simple ideas, namely, that newspapers are important for the democratic political process, that newspapers are constantly fighting each other and fighting for survival, and that there needs to be a way of understanding the nature of the industry so as to be able to help it in some way to survive (and thrive) for the benefit of the democratic political process, if nothing else. Hence the particular concerns of the 1961–62 Royal Commission when faced with the prospect of newspaper closures. But, as many of the extracts show, it is difficult to propose schemes to help the industry and, at the same time, wish to retain a competitive, self-regulated, commercially driven industry.

On this larger canvas, one can find a host of other themes that criss-cross each other. Of these, the concern about the concentration of ownership and the effects of concentration on the diversity of content and plurality of ideas is without doubt a recurring one. The existing rules to guard against excessive concentration (see 5.11–13) are, it seems, easily circumvented by those determined enough to do so.

Another concern has been that of the 'performance of the press'. This is an issue that Royal Commissions have looked into in terms both of content diversity, and of whether newspapers give adequate and truthful coverage of issues and events. Often, newspapers have been criticised for inadequate performances, but since there are no mechanisms by which to force the industry to improve itself, bodies of inquiry do no more than alert readers to such concerns. Given the competitive nature of the newspaper industry, it is difficult to see how a 'social responsibility' model of journalism can be made to sit alongside a deep desire to be secure and profitable.

The final theme that ought to be highlighted – and it is one that was widely debated from the 1960s through to the 1980s – is that of making the industry more efficient and in the process helping it to survive into the future. For many, the way to reach this goal was to invest in the 'new technology' of computerisation so as to cut back on the use of labour power in the production process. However, as several of the quotes show, this was by no means a solution in itself. If the competitive forces remained unchanged, all that would be gained would be a temporary advantage for the more efficient unit. Furthermore, it would not make it cheaper or easier to bring out new titles since the cost of the technology was immense.

The struggle to introduce new technology was fierce and it came at a cost to the unions and to journalists. Only one of the national titles launched in the wake of these changes in the mid-1980s, *The Independent*, survived into the late 1990s, but by then it was in the grip of a well-established newspaper proprietor and living a rather precarious life.

Looking back across the period, then, one is struck by how the concerns of previous Royal Commissions echo each other and how they retell the same stories: of threats to democracy if newspapers fail, of the fear of concentration, of sometimes inadequate performances, of continuing competition, and so on. What they also show is the inability to develop schemes for the industry which are acceptable to all.

The newspaper industry will, therefore, make its way into the twenty-first century with the luggage of past difficulties clinging to its back and the threats from newer news communications technologies, such as thematic television news channels and the internet, forcing it to redefine itself in some new way.

Aspects of press performance

Chapter 5 looks at some key issues which have been of particular concern to the newspaper industry. They add to our understanding of how the industry runs itself and what those working within it can, and cannot, do.

Ownership

Newspapers are controlled in a variety of ways. Sometimes they are owned by a group where the person in charge is able to exercise enormous powers over them (e.g. Robert Maxwell, Rupert Murdoch); sometimes the newspapers are left to their own devices (e.g. as under Roy Thomson); and sometimes they are owned by a trust that acts in a benevolent way (the Scott Trust). These different forms of ownership are highlighted through a selection of extracts which focus on the ways that individuals have pursued different means of controlling newspapers. The main theme to emerge is one of proprietorial power and editorial powerlessness (see 5.1–10).

Media cross-ownership

Newspaper groups have changed in character since the early decades of the twentieth century. As with different proprietorial styles, there are now different types of newspaper groups with many now having important links across media, principally with television. These cross-media links can lead to monopolies or restrictions on diversity of content. Furthermore, because they involve a tie-up between an unregulated industry and a regulated one, rules have been drawn to ensure that the risk of monopolies is reduced and that dominance in particular sectors is not abused. The background to the rules, as well as the most current ones, are highlighted in the selection of extracts in this section (see 5.11–13).

The debates surrounding privacy legislation

The lack of responsibility that newspapers often display when they intrude into the private dimension of the lives of individuals has been a long-standing concern. In an industry that is self-regulated, it is important that the system of self-regulation is robust. From the 1947–49 Royal Commission onwards, there have been attempts to strengthen the system of self-regulation through the Press Council, now the Press Complaints Commission. Yet in spite of the existence

16

of such bodies, of codes of conduct for journalists and editors, and threats from politicians, newspapers – especially the tabloids – have continued to transgress acceptable and responsible forms of journalism. The involvement of the press with the monarchy is perhaps the best known case. And though newspapers have been damned, the threat of legislation remains just that, a threat only (see 5.14–26).

The Lobby: reforming political journalism?
The system of political reporting in Britain has been long shrouded in mystery. Its rules and its practices are a source of much debate. Journalists, nevertheless, have had mixed views about opening up the system to all and of making it more transparent. By the end of 1997, the Labour government had promised to make the system more open and to allow the sources of information – the so-called 'sources close to the Prime Minister' – to be identified more precisely (see 5.26).

The political affiliations or allegiances of newspapers
Until recently, the balance of newspaper preferences had always been in the Conservative Party's favour, but in 1997 *The Sun* changed its traditional allegiance and backed the Labour Party. This tipped the balance a little, but for how long? And has it done any harm to the reputation of Tony Blair, the Labour Prime Minister, to be seen to be closely allied to Rupert Murdoch?

1
Terrestrial television, 1945–1998

Debates about how broadcasting systems should be organised and what they should do throw up recurring themes which focus on the ways in which the goals of broadcasting can best be achieved. This chapter explores these larger and more general questions about how broadcasting systems should be organised and run, and the consequences of different structures on the nature of the broadcasting system and its output.

1.1 The introduction of commercial television: the Beveridge Committee

Radio was still the most important medium of mass communication when the first Committee on Broadcasting was set up in 1949. The Committee's report included a Minority Report by Selwyn Lloyd. This is often cited as one of *the* critical documents in the history of commercial television in that it suggested that there should be a commercial alternative to the BBC.

5. ... the most important question submitted to us is whether it is right that the control and development of this means of informing, educating and entertaining should remain with a single body of men and women. While acknowledging gladly the great gifts and high principles of those in authority at Broadcasting House, I cannot agree that it is in the public interest that all this actual and potential influence should be vested in a public or private monopoly....

9. ... I believe that the only effective safeguard [against the dangers of monopolistic powers] is competition from independent sources.

Without that competition the basic evils and dangers of monopoly will remain....

12. ... I am not attracted by the idea of compulsory uplift achieved by 'the brute force of monopoly' to use Lord Reith's phrase. If people are to be trusted with the franchise, surely they should be able to decide for themselves whether they want to be educated or entertained in the evening. As long as provision is made for those who wish to listen to classical music or plays or poetry readings, etc. I see no reason why there should not be competition for listeners in the rest of the field.... Therefore provided that there is a public service system, with its finances secured, able to set a high standard, to give a lead, and to cater for minorities, I much prefer to leave the rest to the freedom of choice rather than to 'the brute force of monopoly'....

23. Other television corporations. In due course one or more other Companies or Corporations could be licensed to provide the alternative television programmes which sooner or later the public will certainly demand, and which are now technically possible. When that has taken place, it might be desirable to follow the same pattern as with sound broadcasting, a public service non-commercial programme financed by a licence fee and alongside it one or more other agencies financed commercially....

Selwyn Lloyd, Minority Report submitted to the Committee on Broadcasting 1949 (Chairman: Lord Beveridge), London: HMSO, Cmd 8116, January 1951, pp. 201, 203, 205, 209.

1.2   John Reith's defence of the status quo

The Labour government's response to the Committee's report (Cmd 8291, July 1951) only lent support to the continuation of the monopoly. However, the debates about broadcasting continued in 1952 and produced this statement from Lord Reith in defence of the status quo.

What grounds are there for jeopardising this heritage and tradition? Not a single one is even suggested in the White Paper. Why sell it down the river? Do we find leadership and decision in this White Paper; or compromise and expediency – a facing-both-ways? A principle which is absolutely fundamental and cherished is scheduled to be scuttled.... The Government are here on record to scuttle – a betrayal and a surrender; that is what is so shocking and serious; so unnecessary and wrong. Somebody introduced dog-racing into England; we know who, for he is proud of it, and proclaims it *urbie et orbi* in the columns of Who's Who. And somebody introduced Christianity and printing and the uses of electricity. And somebody introduced smallpox, bubonic plague and the Black Death. Somebody is minded now to introduce sponsored broadcasting into this country.

J. Reith, *House of Lords Debates*, 22 May 1952, col. 1297.

1.3 The struggle for commercial television

How was the Minority Report received and what is its place in the struggle for commercial television? H. H. Wilson's *Pressure Group* (1961) provides many of the answers in a rich study of lobbying practices in British politics. Wilson's main interest lay in the question of how a small group of like-minded individuals were able to force through radical change. As to why change came about after the 1951 election, Wilson suggests that the 'arrival of one hundred new Conservative Members' (1961: 79) may form part of the explanation. Their attitude towards broadcasting differed significantly from the attitudes prevalent in the years immediately after the Second World War.

Wilson concludes his introduction with a general critique of television which is just as relevant today as it was nearly forty years ago.

[Selwyn Lloyd's Minority Report became] in 1953 the nominal platform for the dedicated minority which ultimately succeeded in converting the Conservative Parliamentary Party to commercial television. Though Mr Lloyd subsequently supported and worked with the Conservative backbench group, he apparently arrived independently at the conclusions expressed in his minority report....

Even in the first few weeks after the election there was no pervasive enthusiasm within the Conservative Parliamentary Party for the introduction of commercial broadcasting....

There can be no doubt that the initial impetus, as well as the sustained effort to obtain the introduction of a commercial alternative to the BBC came from John Rogers, Charles Orr-Ewing, and John Profumo, all of whom had been elected to Parliament in 1950.... these men, with a few colleagues, organised an informal backbench broadcasting 'Group', which provided the major pressure on the Government throughout this controversy....

Certainly the background and business experience of these individuals insured their sympathy for advertising and commerce, as well as providing access to Parliament for those business interests anxious that their point of view should be considered in the formulation of Conservative broadcasting policy....

One may conclude that the introduction of commercial television must inevitably speed up the commercialization of society, a fact noted by several of the opponents. Ironically, this innovation seemed to many a long step in the direction of 'Americanization' of British society, and it was taken by the Party representing those who had been most vehement in condemning American (i.e. vulgar) influence. Thus the Conservative Party sanctioned a development which, its critics maintained, speeds the movement towards a society which would glorify middle class consumption goals and the commercialisation of all institutional and personal relationships and values.... Many [of the advocates of 'Tory democracy'] were perceptive enough to understand that the subtle and long-term impact of commercial television would re-inforce the political results of the vast expansion of hire-purchase, government subsidised loans for home ownership, the drive to get low income groups to purchase shares of corporate stocks, and the pervasive growth of advertising inspired by motivational research.... With other media, commercial television operates to 'interlace the consumption expectations of their readers and listeners with the interests of their backers and advertisers.... The rise of the consumption-oriented individual of mass society thus sets the stage for the shrinkage of the ideologically oriented nineteenth-century party.' [Kirchheimar, 1957]

H. H. Wilson, *Pressure Group: The Campaign for Commercial Television*, London: Secker & Warburg, 1961, pp. 55, 80–1, 16. (Also quoting from O. Kirchheimar, 'The waning of opposition in parliamentary regimes', *Social Research*, Summer 1957, pp. 127–56.)

1.4   The Conservative government's position on competition in broadcasting

The new Conservative government of 1951 accepted the likelihood of competition in television (paragraph 7, below), but in other respects, for example with regards to the position of the BBC, it was in tune with the previous Labour government's position. Importantly, the creation of competition also led to the creation of an authority to supervise the commercial sector.

THE QUESTIONS OF THE MONOPOLY AND SPONSORED BROADCASTING

4. The successive Licences granted to the B.B.C. have not of themselves established the Corporation as the sole authority for all broadcasting in the United Kingdom. The Corporation have, in fact, enjoyed an exclusive privilege because successive Governments have decided that, although the Postmaster General is empowered by statute to license any number of persons to operate broadcasting stations, he should not license anyone other than the B.B.C.

5. The Government recognise that this effective monopoly has done much to establish the excellent and reputable broadcasting service for which this country is renowned and that the B.B.C. have become an important part of the structure of our national life. Their services must remain intact and the Corporation should be the only broadcasting organisation having any claim on the revenue from broadcasting receiving licences....

6. The question whether broadcasting in the United Kingdom should continue to be entrusted solely to the B.B.C. has much exercised the minds of all who have considered it. The late Government accepted the majority recommendation of the Broadcasting Committee that the Corporation should be continued as the authority responsible for all broadcasting, including television....

7. The present Government have come to the conclusion that in the expanding field of television provision should be made to permit some element of competition when the calls on capital resources at present needed for purposes of greater national importance make this feasible. ...

9. It would be necessary to introduce safeguards against possible abuses, and a controlling body would be required for this purpose,

for regulating the conduct of the new stations, for exercising a general oversight of the programmes and for advising on appropriate matters; the new stations would not be permitted to engage in political or religious broadcasting. Licences for any new stations would be granted (and, if necessary, withdrawn) by the Postmaster General on the advice of this body, subject to reservation by the Government of all rights in time of emergency.

Broadcasting: Memorandum on the Report of the Broadcasting Committee 1949, London: HMSO, Cmd 8550, May 1952, pp. 26–7.

1.5 The Television Act 1954

The 1954 Act established the Independent Television Authority and specified its many duties, including general provisions about programmes, which were to bring the service into line with the guidelines pertaining to BBC programming as well as duties of oversight in respect of advertisements which were to fund the broadcasting system.

3. – (1) It shall be the duty of the Authority to satisfy themselves that, so far as possible, the programmes broadcast by the Authority comply with the following requirements, that is to say –

(a) that nothing is included in the programme which offends against good taste or decency or is likely to encourage or incite to crime or to lead to disorder or to be offensive to public feeling or which contains any offensive representation of or reference to a living person;

(b) that the programmes maintain a proper balance in their subject matter and a high general standard of quality;

(c) that any news given in the programmes (in whatever form) is presented with due accuracy and impartiality; ...

(f) that due impartiality is preserved on the part of the persons providing the programmes as respects matters of political or industrial controversy or relating to current public policy;

(g) ... that no matter designed to serve the interests of any political party is included in the programmes; ...

Rules As to Advertisements

1. The advertisements must be clearly distinguishable as such and recognisably separate from the rest of the programme.

2. The amount of time given to advertising in the programmes shall not be so great as to detract from the value of the programmes as a medium of entertainment, instruction and information.

3. Advertisements shall not be inserted otherwise than at the beginning or the end of the programme or in natural breaks therein, and rules ... shall be observed –

(a) as to the interval which must elapse between any two periods given over to advertisements;

(b) as to the classes of broadcasts ... in which advertisements may not be inserted, and the interval which must elapse between any such broadcast and any previous or subsequent period given over to advertisements.

Television Act 1954, Chapter 55, pp. 486–7, 501.

1.6 A critique of commercial television: Richard Hoggart and the Pilkington Committee on Broadcasting 1960

Associated Rediffusion was the first commercial television company to go on air in September 1955. From the beginning the commercial companies concentrated on providing programmes of popular appeal, and the BBC soon lost its commanding position. In 1958 it saw its share of the audience plummet. In the television 'top ten' ratings for 18 September 1960, there was not one single BBC programme on the list.

The success of commercial television alerted many to the danger of a decline in the quality and range of television programmes. One exponent of that view was Richard Hoggart, who was to play a prominent role as a member of the Pilkington Committee. Hoggart wrote of commercial television that 'we have only to watch the programmes in the peak hours ... for a few evenings to appreciate which way that organisation wants to push this society. They want to push it towards a generalised form of life which looks like the life we have known and for the rest looks nicely acceptable – but whose texture is as little that of a good life as processed bread is like home-baked bread' (quoted in Briggs, 1995: 273).

In Hoggart's work, and in the work of the Pilkington Committee on Broadcasting 1960 (on which he sat), one can find a sustained effort to explore the 'purposes of broadcasting'. The success of commercial television, and the relative failure of the BBC, as well as the prospect of more channels coming on-stream, provided a suitable context for the Committee to try and define the ways in which broadcasting should develop for the benefit of society as a whole.

The Committee was established 'to consider the future of the broadcasting services in the UK' (paragraph 1) at a time when television broadcasting was still in its infancy. Although the BBC had been broadcasting television programmes for some fifteen years, the ITV companies, by contrast, had only been in operation for a mere five. Inevitably, then, the Committee was going to provide a 'first report' on the performance of the ITV companies. But the Committee reflected its time in other ways: there was an extensive consideration of radio broadcasting, a strong belief in retaining control over broadcasting, an obvious concern over portrayals of violence and the effects of television, and a concerted effort to pass judgement on television per se. In this latter respect, the Committee set out those criteria which it could use to pass judgement on television, but in view of its criticisms of ITV, it was not surprising that BBC got the third channel and ITV did not.

34. It is no surprise that the purposes [of broadcasting] should be stated in terms so general. Opposing views were expressed to us on many particular aspects of our task; but there was unanimity on this – that no written formula for good broadcasting is possible. Good broadcasting is a practice, not a prescription.... Though its standards exist and are recognisable, broadcasting is more nearly an art than an exact science. It deals in tastes and values, and is not precisely definable. For this reason, the formal documents could do no more than lay down general precepts and delegate to the responsible authorities the task of translating them into practices recognisable as not less than 'good broadcasting'. It is, therefore, the programmes which are the test of the authorities' success.... We have considered first the product and then the producer, rather than the reverse. It is the listeners and viewers for whom the service is provided; and they are interested primarily in what is offered to them, not in how or by whom it is produced....

96. ... the range of subjects dealt with was too narrow, because within the range there was not sufficient variety in treatment and because the range presented at peak viewing hours was markedly narrower even than the overall range....

99. A trivial approach can consist in a failure to respect the potentialities of the subject matter, no matter what it be, or in a too ready reliance on well-tried themes, or in a habit of conforming to established patterns, or in a reluctance to be imaginatively adventurous....

101. The criticism of triviality as we have described it was that trivial programming was a waste of the medium, and represented a failure to realise its potentialities....

Appraisal of the television service of the BBC
113. We have seen that good television broadcasting may be said to comprise three major elements. First, programme planning and content must respect the right of the public to choose from amongst the widest possible range of subject matter. Second, in every part of this wide range of subject matter there must be a high quality of approach and presentation. Last, and by no means least, since it is of overriding importance, those who handle so powerful a medium must be animated by a sense of its power to influence values and moral standards and by its capacity for enriching the lives of all of us. The broadcasting authorities must care about public tastes and attitudes, in all their manifold variety, and must keep aware of them. They must also keep aware of their capacity to change and develop; they must in this sense give a lead....

Appraisal of the BBC's television service: a summing up
149. The BBC know good broadcasting; by and large, they are providing it. We set out to consider how far the main causes of disquiet and dissatisfaction were attributable to the BBC's television service. The BBC are not blameless; but the causes are not, we find, to any great extent attributable to their service. This is the broad consensus of view revealed by the representations put to us by people and organisations which spoke to us as viewers. Their view is perhaps seen most significantly in this: that whatever criticism they made of television, they nearly all went on to say that, if there were to be an additional television programme, it should be provided by the BBC. We have no hesitation in saying that the BBC command public confidence. There are blemishes, too; mistakes, as there must be of judge-

ment. And we repeat that there was criticism of a more general kind which, we felt, had some substance; that the BBC had lowered their standards in some measure in order to compete with independent television. But our broad conclusion is this; that, within the limits imposed by a single programme, the BBC's television service is a successful realisation of the purposes of broadcasting as defined in the Charter....

Appraisal of the service of independent television: a summing up
207. ... [On ITV] the general judgement is unmistakable: it is that the service falls well short of what a good public service of broadcasting should be....

208. We conclude that the stated views of the Authority on the purposes of broadcasting do not accord with those we have formulated earlier in the Report. The differences are not only of emphasis. The role of the broadcasting organisation, as the Authority interpreted it to us, seemed to lack that positive and active quality which is essential to good broadcasting. We reject, too, its view that television will be shaped by society. A number of factors will operate to shape television, to form the character of the service; but what must figure very largely are the attitudes, the conviction, the motives of those who provide programmes – who plan and produce what we see on our television screens. Their role is not passive; they in turn will be helping, however imperceptibly, to affect society.

209. The disquiet about and dissatisfaction with television are, in our view, justly attributed very largely to the service of independent television. This is so despite the popularity of the service, and the well-known fact that many of its programmes command the largest audiences. Our enquiries have brought us to appreciate why this kind of success is not the only, and is by no means the most important, test of a good broadcasting service. Indeed, it is a success which can be obtained by abandoning the main purposes of broadcasting.... We conclude that the service of independent television does not successfully realise the purposes of broadcasting as defined in the Television Act....

Report of the Committee on Broadcasting 1960 (Chairman: Sir Harry Pilkington), London: HMSO, Cmnd 1753, June 1962, pp. 12–13, 33–4, 37, 46, 67–8.

1.7 Differences between independent television and the BBC television service, 1960

The Pilkington Committee provided a bar chart to illustrate some significant differences between the two organisations.

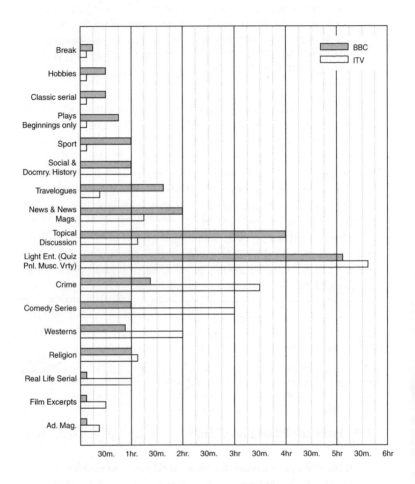

Report of the Committee on Broadcasting 1960 (Chairman: Sir Harry Pilkington), London: HMSO, Cmnd 1753, June 1962, p. 47.

1.8   Tony Benn's views on the BBC, 1964

But committees rarely set the full agenda for policies; changes of government can make some difference to policies but not necessarily a great deal. Tony Benn's stewardship of broadcasting reveals that the Labour government of 1964 – or at least that particular minister – was no 'friend' of the BBC. For example, whilst others may have been happy to see the existing arrangements continue even to the point of imposing restrictions on the 'pirate radio' stations of the 1960s as a way of shoring up the BBC's monopoly, Benn was ready to recognise both the reasons, and the need, for change. Soon after taking over as Postmaster General, he jotted down the 'five questions' which he discussed with radio and television journalists, including the possibility of the BBC taking advertising for a pop music station.

The five questions I discussed with them were:
1. Are we making the most of radio and television in Britain?
2. Have we thought through the impact of technical change on the structure of broadcasting?
3. Does broadcasting offer an adequate publishing outlet or is it for ever to be left to the editors?
4. Do future financing arrangements have to follow the same division between all-licence and all-advertising ...? Or are there other means of financing, or a mixture of the two?
5. Is public service synonymous with monopoly? Is advertising synonymous with commercial broadcasting?

T. Benn, *Out of the Wilderness: Diaries 1963–67*, London: Hutchinson, 1987, entry dated 16 November 1964, p. 187.

1.9   From the Pilkington Committee to the Annan Committee

If the Pilkington Committee found it relatively unproblematic to set out the 'purposes of broadcasting' and to pass judgement on the performance of the broadcasters, the next committee on broadcasting – the Annan Committee – was much more riven by doubt and a lack of certainty. Much had changed in the intervening fifteen or so years. Socially and politically, the country was much more divided: the 'swinging' sixties, the student protests of 1968, the emergence of the race issue, the industrial strife, the women's movement, the changing economic and industrial landscape, all these and many other factors placed the broadcasters in a position which they had not previously confronted.

The perception of change became a cornerstone of contemporary critiques of the media and society. The Annan Committee devoted a whole section to 'The change in the climate of opinion' in Britain.

2.1 ... The questions which the public were now asking about broadcasting were vastly different from those which concerned that Committee [Pilkington]. They were more critical, more hostile and more political....

[Since the Pilkington Committee the] most striking change in broadcasting was brought about by the change during this period in the culture of our country. The ideals of middle class culture, so felicitously expressed by Matthew Arnold a century ago, which had created a continuum of taste and opinion, always susceptible to change and able to absorb the avant-garde within its urban, liberal, flexible principles, found it ever more difficult to accommodate the new expressions of life in the sixties. The new vision of life reflected divisions within society, divisions between classes, the generations and the sexes, between north and south, between the provinces and London, between pragmatists and ideologues. Sometimes the divisions existed but were given new publicity: sometimes they were postulated and then were brought about.... It was during this shift in the nation's culture that the BBC began to recruit in sizeable numbers young production staff to man the second channel ... and inevitably some of the new recruits reflected these ideas in their programmes.

2.27. The shift heightened the tensions between the Broadcasting Authorities and the younger producers, but even more dramatically between the Authorities and the Government....

2.28. Hitherto it had been assumed – apart from the occasional flurry over a programme – that Britain had 'solved' the problem of the political relations of broadcasting to Government, Parliament and public. Now people of all persuasions began to object that many programmes were biased or obnoxious. But some, with equal fervour, maintained that broadcasters were not challenging enough and were cowed by Government and private interests to produce programmes which bolstered up the status quo and concealed how a better society could evolve....

2.30. These are some of the reasons why a new debate about the nature of broadcasting began. It has been put to us that broadcasting should be 'opened up'. At present, so it is argued, the broadcasters have become an overnight elite, more interested in preserving their own organisation intact than in enriching the nation's culture. Dedicated to the outworn concepts of balance and impartiality, how can the broadcasters reflect the multitude of opinions in our pluralist society? Their obsession with obtaining as large a mass audience as possible, so the argument runs, contorts the scheduling of programmes and constricts the creativity of the producers.... These contentions ... [suggest] that we should re-examine the whole structure of broadcasting and the political assumptions on which the British system rests. Fifteen years ago people would have found this astonishing. Just as the ground of the debate about broadcasting has shifted, so have the demands which people make of the broadcasters changed....

Report of the Committee on the Future of Broadcasting (Chairman: Lord Annan), London: HMSO, Cmnd 6753, March 1977, pp. 8, 14–16.

1.10 Annan's way forward

The Annan Committee was clearly in favour of change but for change which broadened the available choice. It sought flexibility of structure, diversity of services, editorial independence, as well as accountability in broadcasting through Parliament, and it could not envisage these things co-existing within the duopoly. Its recommendations were consequently framed with these objectives in mind: creating authorities which would provide for the diversity that was somehow missing in the duopoly. In contrast to the deregulatory turn of the 1980s, the Annan Committee was still wedded to a form of state intervention in the structures of broadcasting in support of some notion of the public good.

7.5. We do not believe that, if we want flexibility and diversity, the present structure of two broadcasting Authorities ... assuming responsibility for all broadcasting services, should continue unaltered until the 1990s. Yet neither do we believe that a multiplication of Authorities all on the same lines is the answer.... Competition in excellence is admirable. But competition solely to gain audiences has less desirable effects. Broadcasting in the United States strongly suggests two conclusions. The first is that virtually unrestricted competition between three broadcasting networks narrows the range of programmes. The second is that competition for the same source of finance lowers programming standards so as to satisfy the lowest common denominator. It also transfers power to the financier, who will select the broadcasting organisation most likely to achieve his ends ... Competition between the Broadcasting Authorities [in Britain] cannot be eliminated.... But the ill effects of competition can be mitigated, and we are recommending structures which we think will help to do this while indicating to each Authority what its special role should be....

Conclusion and Summary of Recommendations
30.1. We were asked to consider the future of broadcasting after 1979. We have three objectives. The first is to preserve British broadcasting as a public service accountable to the public through Parliament.... The second is to devise a new structure for broadcasting ... [for] diversity.... Our third objective is to keep the editorial independence of broadcasting organisations free from the control of political pressure groups and vested interests.

30.2. ... We maintain that the Broadcasting Authority is the institution best fitted to give effect to them. [It is] the best mediator between the broadcasters and the public....

30.3. ... We believe that in future broadcasting services should be provided by establishing more Authorities in regulated diversity.

30.4. Regulated diversity means that each broadcasting Authority is responsible for giving its own type of service. They should not provide exactly the same services nor should they compete for exactly the same source of finance.

Report of the Committee on the Future of Broadcasting (Chairman: Lord Annan), London: HMSO, Cmnd 6753, March 1977, pp. 72–3, 471.

1.11 The Annan Committee on the fourth channel

The Committee had developed its own views on how the fourth channel – the last terrestrial television channel with complete reach across Britain – should be organised and run.

15.16 ... there was one other set of proposals which became for us steadily more attractive because they went to the heart of the organisation of broadcasting.... the most comprehensive scheme came from Mr Anthony Smith who proposed that ... a National Television Foundation should be set up. 'It would supplement existing broadcasting by broadening the input by allowing anyone to bring a project to it ... The Foundation would then play a kind of impresario role, merely allocating resources to some but fitting producers, writers, technicians to others ...'.... There would be 'virtually no employees' only its control mechanism plus 'small, legal, financial and administrative units' ... It would be financed from a number of sources: from a fixed annual sum taken from advertising and from payments by educational authorities ... and from sponsored programmes....

15.18 We are convinced that this is the right approach to the fourth channel. A great opportunity would be missed if the fourth channel were seen solely in terms of extending the present range of programmes.... We see the fourth channel as a challenge to broadcasters.... So we do not see the fourth channel merely as an addition to the plurality of outlets, but as a force for plurality in a deeper sense. Not only could it be a nursery for new forms and new methods of presenting ideas, it could also open the door to a new kind of broadcast publishing....

15.20. A new Authority would have far greater freedom than the IBA to develop a new service on this channel. We recommend that an Open Broadcasting Authority (OBA) should be established.

Report of the Committee on the Future of Broadcasting (Chairman: Lord Annan), London: HMSO, Cmnd 6753, March 1977, pp. 234–6.

1.12 Anthony Smith's proposals for the fourth channel

Anthony Smith's submission to the Annan Committee explored the same sorts of ideas which he had expounded in

The Guardian. Many of these ideas can, with hindsight, be criticised for their *naïveté* and for reflecting the rebellious spirit of the age as well as the general disillusionment with settled arrangements. Here one could, for example, include the proposal that the channel 'would have no regular fixed schedules, and no news bulletins at fixed times to cut up the evening'; and that the channel would be run through 'semi-public discussions' rather than closed and secret meetings.

Nevertheless, the proposals underlined the demand for change and the sense that here was an opportunity to create something new. Incidentally, in his book *Grand Inquisitor*, the broadcaster Robin Day wrote that he had put forward similar proposals for a broadcaster-publisher organisation to the Pilkington Committee but that they had been 'totally ignored' (1989: 183).

There is simply no way in which publishing through the air can be made as free as publishing on pieces of paper. A wavelength belongs to society; it has to be given out and can therefore be withdrawn. What has to be achieved is a form of institutional control wedded to a different doctrine from existing broadcasting authorities, to a doctrine of openness rather than to balance, to expression rather than to neutralization.

An NTF [National Television Foundation] would have virtually no employees and no machinery. It would consist merely of its control mechanism, plus a small legal, financial, administrative secretariat....

We now have a rare opportunity to inaugurate a new channel. The most important single thing we should ensure in deciding (assuming it should be used at all) to whom it should be awarded, is that the channel is placed outside the existing duopoly. It should be forced to develop not from a central apparatus but by using the talent and skill of the country as a whole to produce a new culture of broadcasting, a fresh attitude to content.

What is more, if the channel is placed in the hands of the IBA and the companies it will complete the symmetrical strait-jacket of broadcasting in Britain and perpetuate it: two public institutions would each supervise two channels and they would compete, two by two, for parallel audiences for ever. In other words, awarding the new channel, or even a substantial part of it, to the IBA and the companies would damage broadcasting irreparably. Better not to award it at all than to place it in these particular wrong hands.

A. Smith, *The Shadow in the Cave*, London: Quartet, 1976, pp. 288, 295.

1.13 The Labour government's views on the fourth channel, 1978

The Labour government's White Paper of 1978 adopted the Annan Committee's proposals.

12. A unique opportunity will be missed if the fourth channel is not used to explore the possibilities of programmes which say something new in new ways. The aim will be to widen the choice available to viewers by providing programmes which are interesting and worthwhile in their own right but are not intended to compete with programmes on the existing channels for mass audiences.... As regards the minority interest programmes it would be a mistake to suppose that the minorities in question are invariably small: many of them will comprise millions of people, for example, those who follow or play particular sports or are interested in particular kinds of music or drama. The fourth channel will also provide a significant new outlet for programmes which reflect the diversity of cultures in this country, including the cultures of the ethnic minorities and of newcomers to this country....

13. The use of the fourth channel for programmes of minority interest will also be reflected in the arrangements ... for a Welsh language service to have priority on the fourth channel in Wales....

14. The character of the fourth channel service will be determined not only by the kinds of programmes it contains but also by the sources from which its programmes will be obtained. The Government agrees with the Annan Committee that the fourth channel should include programmes from a wide variety of sources, in particular producers from outside the existing broadcasting organisations.

15. The Government agrees with the Annan Committee that a different kind of service requires a new authority ... an Open Broadcasting Authority (OBA). It will be the new Authority's function to provide and supervise a television service of high quality which informs, educates and entertains, and also fulfils the objectives outlined (above) – that is, a service in which priority is given to:

(a) educational programmes;

(b) programmes catering particularly for tastes and interests which are not adequately catered for on the existing services; and

(c) programmes produced outside the existing broadcasting organisations....

20. ... The Government believes that in order to have an assured financial base, a minority channel of the kind envisaged is bound to need a measure of financial assistance from the Government, at any rate in the early years when the fourth television channel is being launched.... as the fourth channel service becomes established ... the Government will expect the OBA to look to advertising revenues of various kinds to provide ... an important and increasing source of finance for its operation....

Home Office, *Broadcasting*, London: HMSO, Cmnd 7294, 1978, pp. 9, 11–12.

1.14   The Conservative government's Broadcasting Bill, 1980

The Conservative government – elected in 1979 – published its Broadcasting Bill in February 1980. This contained somewhat different proposals for the fourth channel, proposals which changed considerably the planned structure, if not the spirit, of the service. The IBA was given the authority to run Service 2, as it was referred to in the Bill.

3.–(1) As regards the programmes (other than advertisements) broadcast in Service 2 it shall be the duty of the Authority –

(a) to ensure that the programmes contain a suitable proportion of matter calculated to appeal to tastes and interests not generally catered for by Service 1;

(b) ... to ensure that a suitable proportion of the programmes are of an educational nature;

(c) to encourage innovation and experiment in the form and content of programmes,

and generally to give Service 2 a distinctive character of its own.

4.(2) The Authority shall arrange for the following activities involved in providing programmes (other than advertisements) for broadcasting in Service 2 to be performed by a subsidiary of the Authority formed by them for the purpose, namely –

(a) obtaining and assembling the necessary material; and

(b) such of the other activities involved in providing such programmes as appear to the Authority appropriate.

Broadcasting Bill 139, February 1980, pp. 3–4.

1.15   William Whitelaw's views on the Annan Committee

> William Whitelaw, who was in charge of broadcasting in the first few years of the incoming Conservative government, accepted the main arguments of the Annan Committee, though, as he records, he disagreed with its recommendations.

The Annan Report underlined the importance of the public service responsibilities of broadcasters and the need to secure a balance of programming that responded to minority audiences as well as to a commercially driven mass market.... It proposed that in bringing into operation the then unused 'fourth channel' we should look to create something different from the existing BBC and IBA....

I strongly agreed with all these conclusions. I was less happy, however, with the structures ... proposed.... It seemed to me from the outset quite unnecessary to create these major new bureaucracies.... The case was not for their replacement by a new structure but rather for strengthening the existing system and extending it to other areas....

... the main feature of the (Broadcasting) Act was the creation of Channel 4. I suppose there is no decision that I made in my political career that has had more of an impact on the daily life of families in Britain. One of my main reasons for rejecting [the] proposal for an Open Broadcasting Authority was ... that [it] could never be financially viable. There would have been clear risks in creating an authority directly appointed, and funded to a substantial degree, by Government. I wanted to create a channel that would foster greater, rather than lesser, independence and variety in broadcasting.

W. Whitelaw, *The Whitelaw Memoirs*, London: Headline Books, 1990, pp. 286–9.

1.16 The Peacock Committee on Financing the BBC, 1985

Channel 4 was the last national terrestrial channel available in Britain. Channel 5, which came on air in March 1997, reaches about 70 per cent of the British population. Between these two events much happened which was to change irrevocably the face of British broadcasting. The advent of cable television, followed by that of satellite television, altered the 'ecology' of broadcasting which had characterised the period up to the mid-1980s. Not only were there now new services being planned almost daily, but also the funding structures of these services were different from those of the past. Inevitably, the new arrivals forced the incumbents to adapt and to reassess their futures. It was this rapidly changing scene into which the last major inquiry into broadcasting, the Peacock Committee, was set up in 1985.

3. Why is it right to look at a system of financing the BBC which has been in operation for so long and which has been endorsed by every committee commissioned to review it? A system of this kind cannot be expected to last for ever. People's needs and desires change and so do the opportunities for meeting or satisfying them. Practices widely accepted during one decade may become quite inappropriate in the next, in which different social conditions may prevail and different technological considerations apply. No political decision as complex and detailed as that which determines the structure of broadcasting can be right for all time. It must be reviewed in the light of changing circumstances....

5. ... Originally the scarcity of airwaves made it necessary for their allocation and use to be policed. But we are now in a period of unusually rapid technological advance in broadcasting.... To consider the BBC as if it will continue with something like half of all the small number of channels available is to fail to grasp the nature of changes which are already taking place and whose intensification seems irresistible....

7. ... Given the current technical and institutional framework and the likely developments in the future, how can British broadcasting be financed in such a way as to bring the greatest enjoyment and pleasure to as many viewers and listeners as possible while at the same time fulfilling some public service obligation? ...

The General Problems of Broadcasting Finance
124. It is a good general principle that any service to the public should be designed to promote its satisfaction. If this principle is to govern the provision of a service it can be shown that, provided certain conditions are fulfilled, the public are best served if able to buy the amount of the service required from suppliers who compete for custom through price and quality. In addition, the stimulus of competition provides further benefits to the public through the incentive given to offer new and improved services. It is frequently argued, however, that these 'certain conditions' cannot be fulfilled in the case of broadcasting services and that, therefore, the 'competitive model' is irrelevant to broadcasting policy. Therefore, the observed intervention by government in broadcasting, so it is claimed, is amply justified.

125. The first condition requires acceptance of the proposition that the consumer is the best judge of his/her own interests. Those who oppose this proposition use four closely-related arguments.

126. The first is that consumers often don't know what the relation is between what they buy and the satisfaction that they will derive from the purchase.... This argument does not cut much ice with the Committee, for in the case of broadcast programmes, 'mistakes' in viewing can easily be rectified without major cost to the consumer. Provided that pricing of broadcasting services is possible and there is a choice of such services, then the consumer can learn very quickly how to get the best value for money.

127. The second argument contends that consumers' tastes are not formed by consciously conducted trial and error processes, but by 'outside' forces, notably by advertisers who can manipulate consumer choices.... Within the context of the Committee's task, it implies that replacing the licence fee by advertising revenue for the BBC would not be in the interests of viewers and listeners.

128. Supporters of a third argument contend that even if consumers are freely-acting agents who are aware of what they are doing, they do not automatically choose the pattern of goods and services which is in their best interests.... The principle behind this argument clearly appeals to those who regard broadcasting as a public service designed to influence and not merely to reflect the public's preferences for programmes. Its acceptance would clearly mean that a free market in broadcasting services, if technically possible, should not be encouraged. It brings out very clearly the point that any decision on

how broadcasting services should be financed must embody value judgements....

129. A fourth contends that individuals may derive a general satisfaction from the provision of goods and services to the community at large which is quite distinct, though admittedly difficult to distinguish from their own immediate enjoyment of them.... We give reasons later why we are persuaded that this argument offers a good case for public financing of some broadcasting services which arguably confer such general benefits on the community.

130. The second condition for the operation of the free market requires that the goods or service can be priced, for otherwise the supplier will not be able to recoup his costs from those who wish to purchase it....

196. The duopoly system ensures secure forms of financing for both the BBC, through the licence fee, and for the independent sector as a whole, so long as advertising 'slots' are limited. This security is claimed to be in the public interest because it gives the two parts of the system 'peace to plan' without undue political interference and helps them to fulfil their public service obligation.... At the same time as providing secure funding, it could be claimed that, as distinct from a pure monopoly of broadcasting, the duopoly system adds a competitive edge to the process of programme development which would otherwise be lacking. This, too could redound to the benefit of the listener and viewer by enlarging the choice of new programmes alongside those programmes which are clearly designed to maximise audiences.

197. At the same time, the Committee has to take account of features of duopoly which make it likely that satisfaction of the consumer is not the driving force behind the activities of the producers ... notably the doubts expressed about freedom of entry into programming and the impetus given to maximising audience volume as a method for protecting both major sources of revenue....

209. Before addressing alternative ways of funding the BBC, we feel we must first say a word about the status quo.... The evidence we received suggested that the present system:

(i) is regressive in that the licence fee is a kind of poll tax which all owners of TV sets must pay independent of wealth or income;

(ii) is potentially unfair in that, in theory, owners of TV sets might prefer to watch ITV only;

(iii) is expensive to administer and is therefore an inefficient use of resources;

(iv) appears to require excessive increases in the licence fee because the licence fee is increased only every three years;

(v) encourages evasion of payment of the licence fee, because costs of detection are high and penalties for detection relatively low;

(vi) does not seek to define ... the service which is to be paid for by the licence fee nor is any evaluation of the performance of the BBC in meeting its objectives undertaken;

(vii) implies a degree of political control because the level of the licence fee is set by the Home Secretary ...;

(viii) means that in effect the ordinary licence payers are providing a subsidy for hotel proprietors ... because of the present arrangement for hotels ...

210. Nevertheless, a number of those submitting evidence felt that the licence fee had much to commend it. The licence fee system, they said:

(i) is a secure form of financing for the BBC;

(ii) gives a good deal of freedom from political control;

(iii) preserves the independence of the BBC from other influences;

(iv) maintains a direct relationship between the BBC and the consumers, and

(v) enables the BBC to produce programmes of high quality covering a wide range of subjects.

243. The conclusion is that, paradoxically, the status quo ... represents an unstable situation. If cable and satellite services develop to the extent that they begin to compete significantly for audiences then this will either have an impact on the BBC's programming policy (in order to maintain its audience share) or will make justification of the licence fee politically difficult (because of its declining audience share). If cable and satellite services do not develop the evidence is that ITV revenue will grow at a high rate. It seems doubtful if the aspirations of the BBC could be fulfilled without changes in the BBC's revenue structure....

592. Our own conclusion is that British broadcasting should move towards a sophisticated market based on consumer sovereignty. That is a system which recognises that viewers and listeners are the best ultimate judge of their own interests, which they can best satisfy if they have the option of purchasing the broadcasting services they require from as many alternative sources of supply as possible. There will always be a need to supplement the direct consumer market by

public finance for programmes of a public service kind ... supported by people in their capacity as citizens and voters but unlikely to be commercially self-supporting in the view of the broadcasting entrepreneurs....

596. It follows from our concept of consumer sovereignty that we reject the commercial laissez-faire model, which is based on a small number of broadcasters competing to sell audiences to advertisers. Such a system neither achieves the important welfare benefits theoretically associated with a fully functioning market, nor meets the British standards of public accountability for the private use of public assets. Furthermore, so long as the number of television channels is limited, and there is no direct consumer payment, collective provision and regulation of programmes does provide a better simulation of a market designed to reflect consumer preferences than a policy of laissez-faire....

598. Our consumer sovereignty model is, of course, an ideal, a standard and a goal....

608. The following table sets out the three stages we envisage ... as a guide ...

Table 12.1: The Three Stages

STAGE	LIKELY BROADCASTING DEVELOPMENT	POLICY REGIME
1	Satellite and cable develop, but most viewers and listeners rely on BBC, ITV and independent local radio	Indexation of ... licence fee
2	Proliferation of ... systems, channels and payment methods	Subscription replaces main part of licence fee
3	Indefinite number of channels. Pay-per-view ... available. Technology reduces cost of multiplicity of outlets and of charging methods	Multiplicity of choice leading to full broadcasting market

A Public Service provision will continue through all three stages.

Report of the Committee on Financing the BBC (Chairman: Professor Alan Peacock), London: HMSO, Cmnd 9824, 1986, pp. 133–6.

1.17   Embarrassing the government?

The Peacock Committee went beyond its narrow and defined remit. This, according to one of its members, caused some embarrassment to the government.

The main reason for Government embarrassment was that in putting forward the idea of a free broadcasting market without censorship, Peacock exposed many of the contradictions in the Thatcherite espousal of market forces. In principle, Mrs Thatcher and her supporters are all in favour of de-regulation, competition and consumer choice. But they are also even more distrustful than traditionalist Tories such as Douglas Hurd [then Home Secretary] of plans to allow people to listen and watch what they like, subject only to the law of the land. They espouse the market system but dislike the libertarian value judgements involved in its operation: value judgements which underlie the Peacock report.

The worth of the report does not in the end depend on how many of its recommendations are accepted by a particular government. It lies in the fact that it planted the idea of a broadcasting market akin to publishing, which will flower in its time.

S. Brittan, 'The fight for freedom in broadcasting', *Political Quarterly* 58(1), 1987, p. 4.

1.18   The public service idea in British broadcasting

For many, the Peacock Committee was part of a concerted attack on the BBC and the values it sought to defend. One group of (mainly) academics was brought together by the (now defunct) Broadcasting Research Unit to try to define, and defend, the qualities of public service broadcasting in Britain. A more difficult question – which remains unanswered – is whether the commercial television sector is also a public service broadcaster? (See also 1.27 below.)

The burden of this booklet is that the purposes served by the main provisions of public service broadcasting in Britain go far beyond the policing of a shortage, serve far more important democratic aims and that, though the structure we have is not perfect nor perfectly operated, in general it has served us extremely well; that the continuance of its aims cannot be ensured simply by the operation of market mechanisms; and that, no matter how many outlets for delivery systems the new technologies offer, the essential elements of public service broadcasting should be retained. They are a unique device serving our highest interests and are by now an integral part of the social fabric. If they are lost we shall be diminished as a nation.

Main Principles

1. Universality: Geographic – broadcast programmes should be available to the whole population.

2. Universality of Appeal – broadcast programmes should cater for all interests and tastes.

3. Minorities, especially disadvantaged minorities, should receive particular provision.

4. Broadcasters should recognise their special relationship to the sense of national identity and community.

5. Broadcasting should be distanced from all vested interests, and in particular from those of the government of the day.

6. Universality of Payment – one main instrument of broadcasting should be directly funded by the corpus of users.

7. Broadcasting should be structured so as to encourage competition in good programming rather than competition for numbers.

8. The public guidelines for broadcasting should be designed to liberate rather than restrict the programme makers.

Broadcasting Research Unit, *The Public Service Idea in British Broadcasting: Main Principles*, Luton: John Libbey, 1985–86, Contents.

1.19 The response to Peacock: the 1988 White Paper

The response to the Peacock report indicated that it was unlikely to be adopted wholesale. Yet many of its recommendations were taken up or formed part of other discussions. These included: the indexing of the licence fee, the 25 per cent quota for independent producers on terrestrial television, the competitive tender for allocating ITV franchises, the performance review of ITV contractors, Channel 4 selling its own advertising time, and a review of the future telecommunications system.

The 1988 White Paper *Broadcasting in the '90s: Competition, Choice and Quality* (Cm 517, November 1988) left no one in doubt that the direction of development was towards a much more liberal regime for broadcasting, though perhaps not as liberal as the Peacock Committee would have desired, with the viewers and listeners being given a greater degree of freedom to choose from the slowly expanding menu of services.

1.2 ... The Government's aim is to open the doors so that individuals can choose for themselves from a wider range of programmes and types of broadcasting.... a more open and competitive broadcasting market can be attained without detriment to programme standards and quality. Its single biggest advantage will be to give the viewer and listener a greater choice and a greater say. The Government is also clear that there need be no contradiction between the desire to increase competition and widen choice and concern that programme standards on good taste and decency should be maintained.

1.3 ... The main [proposals] are these:

– ... the authorisation of a fifth channel ...

– The present ITV system will be replaced by a regionally based Channel 3 with positive programming obligations but also greater freedom to match its programming to market conditions.

– ... Channel 4 ... advertising ... [will be] sold separately ...

– The UK's two remaining Direct Broadcasting by Satellite frequencies will be advertised ...

– Viewers will continue to be able to receive other satellite services directly ...

– ... the Independent Television Commission (ITC) will [replace] the Independent Broadcasting Authority (IBA) ...

– The BBC will continue as the cornerstone of public service broadcasting. The Government looks forward to the eventual replacement of the licence fee which will, however, continue for some time to come.

– The part played by Independent producers ... will grow ...

Broadcasting in the '90s: Competition, Choice and Quality, London: HMSO, Cm 517, November 1988, pp. 1–2.

1.20 The Broadcasting Act 1990

By the time of the Broadcasting Act of 1990, many of these developments had taken place, though some had turned out somewhat differently than had been expected (see 2.24–26). One significant aspect of the 1990 Broadcasting Act is that it changed the relationship of the regulator (the to-be-established ITC) to the individual Channel 3 (formerly ITV) contractors. Henceforth, the ITC would grant the licence to an individual contractor and it would then be up to the contractor to ensure that it met the conditions and requirements as set out in the licence. In this respect, the system was more transparent than before and the ITC had to set out clearly what was expected of contractors. The annual Performance Review by the ITC was the mechanism designed to check up on the performance of the contractors.

Other aspects of the Act are noteworthy. First, it established the competitive tendering system for Channel 3 contractors; second, it lessened the Channel 3 providers' commitment to the provision of current affairs programming; and third, it set out how the ITC should regulate the developing satellite services. Finally, it also dealt with the 25 per cent quota for independent productions on all television services, including the BBC's.

[Applications for Channel 3 licences have to be accompanied by]

(3) (a) the fee ...

(b) the applicant's proposals for providing a service ...

(f) the applicant's cash bid in respect of the licence....

(7) ... 'cash bid' ... means an offer to pay to the Commission a specified amount of money in respect of the first complete calendar year....

16. (2) Where the service provided under the licence is a regional Channel 3 service, the requirements ... are –

(a) that a sufficient amount of time is given in the programmes included in the service to news programmes and current affairs programmes which (in each case) are of high quality and deal with both national and international matters, and that such news programmes are broadcast at intervals throughout the period for which the service is provided and, in particular, at peak viewing times;

(b) that a sufficient amount of time is given in the programmes included in the service to programmes (other than news and current affairs programmes) which are of high quality;

(c) that a sufficient amount of time is given in the programmes so included –

(i) to a suitable range of regional programmes ...

(ii) ... to a suitable range of programmes for each of the different parts of the area ...

(e) that a sufficient amount of time is given ... to religious programmes and programmes intended for children;

(f) that (taken as a whole) the programmes so included are calculated to appeal to a wide variety of tastes and interests; ...

17.–(1) ... the Commission shall, after considering all the cash bids submitted ..., award the licence to the applicant who submitted the highest bid.

(2) Where two or more applicants for a particular licence have submitted cash bids specifying an identical amount ... the Commission shall invite those applicants to submit further cash bids in respect of that licence ...

(3) The Commission may disregard the requirements imposed by subsection (1) and award the licence to an applicant who has not submitted the highest bid if it appears to them that there are exceptional circumstances which make it appropriate for them to award the licence to that applicant.

(4) ... the Commission may regard the following circumstances as exceptional circumstances ...

(a) that the quality of the service proposed by such an applicant is exceptionally high, and

(b) that the quality of that proposed service is substantially higher than the quality of the service proposed –

(i) by the applicant who has submitted the highest bid, or

(ii) ... by each of the applicants who have submitted equal highest bids; ...

Broadcasting Act 1990, pp. 13–17.

1.21 The competitive franchising system

Applications for the regional programming licences were invited in February 1991, and in October 1991 the ITC announced the winners of the ten-year Channel 3 licences. The discrepancies in the cash bids were apparent.

Area	Awarded to	Cash bid (£ 1993 prices)
Borders	Border TV plc	52,000
Central Scotland	Scottish TV plc	2,000
Channel Islands	Channel TV plc	1,000
East, West & South Midlands	Central Independent TV plc	2,000
East of England	Anglia TV Ltd	17,804,000
London Weekday	Carlton TV Ltd	43,170,000
London Weekend	LWT (Holdings) plc	7,850,000
North of Scotland	Grampian TV plc	720,000
North-East England	Tyne Tees Television plc	15,057,000
North-West England	Granada TV Ltd	9,000,000
Northern Ireland	Ulster TV plc	1,027,000
South and South-East England	Meridian Broadcasting Ltd	36,523,000
South-West England	Westcountry TV Ltd	7,815,000
Wales and the West of England	HTV Group plc	20,530,000
Yorkshire	Yorkshire TV Ltd	37,700,000

National Breakfast-Time
There were three applicants: Daybreak Television Limited; Sunrise Television Limited; and TV-am plc.... all three would comply with the requirements specified in ... the Broadcasting Act 1990. Sunrise Television has been awarded the licence. The amount of [its] cash bid was £34,610, 000.... TV-am's ... was £14,125,000. Daybreak has not given agreement for its cash bid to be disclosed.

ITC News Release, 16 October 1991, pp. 3, 8.

1.22 Mourning the loss of TV-am

Ironically, the person who was most responsible for setting up the competitive tendering for franchises, Mrs Thatcher, turned out to be one of the people to regret its consequences.

The Guardian revealed extracts from a letter she had written to Bruce Gyngell, chief executive of TV-am.

'I am only too painfully aware that I [underlined] was responsible for the legislation,' she wrote to Bruce Gyngell, chief executive of TV-am, where her daughter Carol works.

'When I see how some of the other licences have been awarded I am mystified [also underlined] that you did not receive yours and heart-broken. You of all people have done so much for the whole of television – there seems to be no attention to that.' ...

At a stroke Mrs Thatcher has undermined the credibility of the system and the careful months of work of the ITC, which tried to do its best with the difficult job bequeathed it. Senior ministers were acutely embarrassed by her outburst against the consequences of the legislation for which she and her Chancellor, Nigel Lawson, were responsible....

Mrs Thatcher saw TV-am, the most profitable company in the ITV network, as a model for the others, which she attacked as the 'last bastion of restrictive practices'. She warmly welcomed Mr Gyngell's victory over striking technicians in 1988 – television's equivalent of Rupert Murdoch's sprint to Wapping....

'Thatcher repudiates TV auction', *The Guardian*, 18 October 1991, p. 1.

1.23 The future of the BBC

But if the changes to Channel 3 (including changes in the rules regarding ownership, see 5.14), Channel 4 and Channel 5 were significant both structurally and in terms of their pro-gramming in a more competitive age, several documents released in the early 1990s pointed to a changing media con-text for the BBC also. The Department of National Heritage published its consultation document, *The Future of the BBC*, in November 1992 (Cm 2098) and this was soon followed by the BBC's own response, *Extending Choice: The BBC's Role in the Broadcasting Age*, later in the same year.

Once the consultation exercise was complete, the depart-ment released its proposals. *The Future of the BBC: Serving the Nation, Competing World-Wide* (Cm 2621, July 1994) set out the government's thinking.

Future role of the BBC

1.1 The Government believes that the BBC should continue to be the United Kingdom's main public service broadcaster. Its primary role should be making and broadcasting programmes for audiences throughout the country.

1.2 However, the next 10 to 15 years will bring rapid and exciting changes in broadcasting. New technologies are emerging and the boundaries between broadcasting and telecommunications and other media are becoming blurred....

1.3 The Government believes the BBC should be able to evolve into an international multi-media enterprise, building on its present commercial services for audiences in this country and overseas....

Commercial activities

1.11 The BBC should expand its commercial activities in the United Kingdom and overseas, and should continue to be able to join with private sector partners to achieve this. Its international services should contribute to improving the United Kingdom's competitiveness in world markets for audio-visual services....

Finance

1.17 The BBC should keep the licence fee as the main source of finance for its public services for at least five years. Funding from the licence fee should be reviewed before the end of 2001.

Department of National Heritage, *The Future of the BBC: Serving the Nation, Competing World-Wide*, London: HMSO, Cm 2621, July 1994, pp. 1, 2, 3.

1.24   The issues for the future: Channel 4

In the early 1990s Channel 4 waged a battle to redefine its relationship to the ITV companies (Channel 3). When launched, Channel 4 was funded by the ITV companies, who in return sold advertising on the Channel. In 1993 Channel 4 was permitted to sell its own advertising but only within the terms of the so-called 'funding formula' which maintained its relationship to ITV. Under the formula, Channel 4 would give the ITV companies 50 per cent of any revenue above the 14 per cent of terrestrial advertising revenue. This cost Channel 4 dear – an estimated £300 million in 1997 – and led to wrangles within the commercial television sector. In 1997 Chris Smith, the Secretary of State for Culture, Media and Sport, launched a consultation exercise which proposed to 'broaden and strengthen' Channel 4's public service commitments – it had gained a reputation for success through importation of programming – at the same time as doing away with the 'funding formula'. (Revisions to the original Channel 4 documents are in italic.)

STATEMENT OF PROGRAMME POLICY
2. The Statutory Programme Remit

The *1990 Broadcasting Act* ... says that Channel 4 programmes 'should contain a suitable proportion of matter calculated to appeal to tastes and interests not generally catered for by Channel 3 and that innovation in the form and content of those programmes [should be] encouraged'. It goes on to say that the Channel 4 Service should have a 'distinctive character'. *It is now recognised that Channel 4 is a public service broadcaster with its own culture, history and sense of purpose which also seeks to define its role in a multi-channel environment in relation to all channels and not ITV alone. It provides public service and creative competition for the BBC....*

4. The Purpose of Channel 4

The Channel 4 Service is not expected to be a mass audience channel though some of its programmes will always aim to attract large numbers. It will foster the new and experimental in television. It will encourage pluralism, provide a favoured place for the untried and encourage innovation ... in style, content, ... perspective *and talent on and off the screen.* Its search for a distinctive character implies different editorial choices at different times since it clearly must take account of what other channels are doing.... *This* provides the chance to introduce new talent, to reaffirm creative alliances or bring together fresh ones, and to develop ideas for which the existing terrestrial services and ... satellite *and cable* services cannot find a place. *The old verities – experiment, innovation, originality and diversity – should be the touchstone now as they have been in the past....*

16. Original Production

Channel 4's programme ... commissioning policy will ... be driven only by the merit of individual programme ideas.... *In commissioning original programmes, Channel 4 will strive to reach targets of at least 55% from 1998, increasing to 60% from 1999, of total programming that is originated by Channel 4. Within peak time (1800 hours to 2230) the Channel will expect that at least 70% of its transmitted hours will be originated programmes. The Channel will show the broadest and the best of acquired material from around the world....*

22. Funding
The termination of the funding formula provisions ... will release funds to Channel 4 to deploy on its services. The Channel is committed to allocating the funds to UK film and programme production and training as well as in meeting its new digital commitment....

23. Summary
...Channel 4 should aspire to be the television broadcaster that is most likely to explore new ideas and connect with new ways of thinking. The Channel 4 Service ... can and should continue to make *a* contribution to ... *a* plural and democratic society ...

ITC News Release, Public Consultation Launched on Revisions to Channel 4 Licence, 24 October 1997.

1.25 The issues for the future: funding

With Channel 4 effectively separated from Channel 3, and Channel 5 in operation from March 1997, the terrestrial services menu was complete by the end of the century. The most significant question – that of the future of the licence fee – was shunted into the next century. By that time, though, the settlements arrived at in the 1980s and 1990s would no longer be tenable. Part of the reason for this was the advent and popularity of the satellite services. Another reason was that the future promised even more services in the form of both digital terrestrial and digital satellite services. But, as always, the questions lurking behind all these developments related to finance.

In their submission to the National Heritage Committee, the consultants Booz-Allen and Hamilton identified six major issues. Three issues concerned Programme Rights Controls,

Changing Programming Focus ('there will be a shift in the sourcing and mix of programmes shown') and the Worsening Trade Balance ('from £100 million in 1991 to up to £640 million in 2000'). The other three were more general yet they contained some telling signs of impending problems.

Regulation
Legislation, and deregulation in particular, has been a major driver in restructuring the broadcasting market.... The Government should be aware of their influence over the market and their responsibility in ensuring that future legislation is appropriate in shaping the changing broadcasting industry.

Shifting Power Base
The power base is shifting away from ITV and advertising funded television to BSkyB and pay television. By 1996 BSkyB could have revenues almost equal to all the ITV companies put together; by 2000 it is estimated to have revenues of £1.7 billion compared to ITV's £1.5 billion.... Currently the new DTH [Direct-to-Home, i.e. satellite] channels are largely exempt from the programme, origin and cross-media ownership rules. The changing power base raises the issues of whether subscription television should share, or even take over, this responsibility.

Globalisation
UK players ... are being overtaken and overshadowed by the global media corporations that make, distribute and deliver film and television software all over the world....

National Heritage Committee, *Minutes of Evidence,* London: HMSO, Session 1993–94, HCP 77-II, pp. 1–2.

1.26 The advent of digital television

By the mid-1990s, digital broadcasting was being heralded as the means to sheer abundance of channels. Digital terrestrial broadcasting would increase the menu by a score or so services, whilst digital satellite television would create hundreds of channels. What would be shown on these services was not entirely clear, although some clues were ever-present: dedicated sports services, more news services, more pay-per-view (ppv) film services, and the like. The Broadcasting Act of 1996 set the framework for this change and for other changes.

An Act to make new provision about the broadcasting in digital form of television and sound programme services and the broadcasting in that form on television and radio frequencies of other services; to amend the Broadcasting Act 1990; to make provision about rights to televise sporting or other events of national interest; to amend in other respects the law relating to the provision of television and sound programme services; to provide for the establishment and functions of a Broadcasting Standards Commission and for the dissolution of the Broadcasting Complaints Commission and the Broadcasting Standards Council; to make provision for the transfer to other persons of property rights and liabilities of the BBC relating to their transmission network; and for connected purposes.

Broadcasting Act 1996, p. 1.

2

The end of scarcity: cable, satellite and telecommunications

In the early post-war period, any discussion of cable (or relay) systems was likely to concern radio, not television, and its role was very much as a carrier of the BBC's signals. Initially developed as a means of enabling better radio reception, the radio relay services of the 1920s flourished despite moves to stall their developments on the grounds that they were usurping the monopoly over all broadcasting matters vested in the BBC. The fear that such services would also introduce listeners to new things (e.g. from overseas) and so upset the programme policy imposed by Reith's BBC ensured that their development would be curtailed. Similar fears were expressed after 1945 by the BBC *and* the ITV companies when the radio relay operators turned their minds away from radio and to television.

2.1 Cable systems: the threat to the BBC monopoly in the 1950s

In 1951 the first relay (cable) television was introduced in the city of Gloucester. Though the operators were looking forward to using their systems for television, the Beveridge Committee on Broadcasting (1949) continued to ask questions which reflected pre-war concerns.

First, should they be taken over by some public authority and operated as a public service, or should they be allowed to continue under licence as private enterprises working for profit? Second, if taken over as a public service, by what public authority should they be operated?... Third, what conditions should be imposed in the licence as to the operation of the relay exchanges?...

[The restrictions] limit the relay exchanges to reception and distribution of programmes, forbid origination of programmes, forbid distribution of political, social or religious propaganda or results of sweepstakes, forbid receipt by the licensee of money or other consideration for receiving and distributing particular programmes, and require the licensee to include a certain proportion of BBC programmes in his distribution....

... where two alternative channels are provided [by the relay operators] one must be used to carry BBC programmes at all times when available, while the other must carry BBC programmes for 75 per cent of the time, and that where three or more channels are provided, two must carry BBC programmes at all times when they are available. The suggestion of the BBC was that since a third alternative is now available in the Third Programme, the licence might be amended to provide that where four or more circuits are provided three of them should carry a BBC programme when available. Most of us are opposed to this suggestion. A listener with an ordinary receiving set is not bound to the BBC programmes at all.

The other suggestion ... [is] that inclusion of [commercial] broadcasts in the programmes offered by relay exchanges should not be allowed.... If the operators of relay exchanges find that they can make their systems more attractive to the listeners by including commercial broadcasts from abroad ... we doubt whether there is justification for imposing on the relay listeners restrictions which would not apply to them as ordinary listeners. The Relay System should be regarded as one way – though admittedly a small one – of introducing variety and experiment in meeting the needs of the listening public.

Report of the Broadcasting Committee 1949 (Chairman: Lord Beveridge), London: HMSO, Cmd 8116, January 1951, pp. 113–15.

2.2 Establishing the principle of choice and competition via relay (cable) television, 1961

Though many bodies submitted proposals for pay or subscription television, few of these bodies had cable or relay interests. The attraction lay in the possibility of offering different, and new, services to viewers.

(a) There is a need for another television service providing not only a higher standard of entertainment, but also a real alternative to the present two services.

(b) This can only be achieved by a Pay Television service, i.e. the viewer being able to choose and pay for the programmes he or she wants.

(c) BHE are prepared to operate a Pay Television service transmitted by wire or over-the-air. There is, however, a strong case for such a service in the first instance to be provided by wire.

(d) Only one standardised wire system should be used throughout the country. This system should be *licensed and controlled by the GPO*....

(g) A Pay Television service should be free of financial control by existing television interests, and theatre and cinema operating companies.

(h) It should derive its revenue exclusively from the voluntary viewer and have no advertising revenue.

(i) Pay Television must not interfere with the availability to all television services of certain national events and party political broadcasts....

British Home Entertainment Ltd, *Subscription Television: Memorandum to the Committee on Broadcasting 1960* (Chairman: Sir Harry Pilkington), London: HMSO, Paper No. 214, July 1961, p. 1057.

2.3 Different perspectives on the threat of the relay services, 1961

By 1960, cable television had been transformed from, as the broadcasters saw it, a useful and controlled method for transmitting signals in bad reception areas to a means of communication which threatened the structure of commercial television in Britain. What the commercial broadcasters feared was the relay operators' ability to import signals from one regional television area into another and so totally undermine the regional structure of commercial television. Related concerns included the ability of operators to import signals from the Continent, and the potential for operators to substitute commercial television's advertisements with their own selection. A very different concern which also surfaced was that of subscription or pay-television (see 2.2).

The established broadcasters continued to press for controls and restrictions (first extract), whilst the Relay Association was pressing for the introduction of subscription television (second extract).

... the relay companies are now urging that they should be relieved from their undertaking [to distribute to subscribers all ITA programmes receivable in their own area by terrestrial means] and advocating that the undertaking is no longer necessary for the protection of the [ITA] contractors.... The maintenance of this undertaking is vital to the whole structure of television.

Associated British Picture Company, *Evidence to the Committee on Broadcasting 1960* (Chairman: Sir Harry Pilkington), London: HMSO, Cmd 1753, June 1961, pp. 622–3.

There is a demand among relay subscribers for more television and sound programmes. Additional programmes should be financed on a commercial basis. There should be no increase in the domestic licence fee.

Consideration should be given to the use of the surplus channel space provided in relay systems for the purposes of introducing subscription television by wire. The extent to which such systems have been and are being extended secures a considerable potential audience, and a subscription service should be provided on an economical basis employing the spare channel capacity of the systems.

Relay Services Association of Great Britain, *Summary of Submission: Evidence to the Committee on Broadcasting 1960* (Chairman: Sir Harry Pilkington), London: HMSO, Paper No. 223, December 1960, p. 1089, paras 13–14.

2.4   The Pilkington Committee, cable television and the 'purposes of broadcasting'

The Pilkington Committee was not swayed by submissions to develop new services since it felt that, on balance, pay televi-

sion would be unable 'to realise the purposes of broadcasting'.

[Would such services] in themselves and in their effect on existing
services, naturally make for the realisation of the purposes of broadcasting; or be so controlled as to ensure that those purposes will be
realised?

The dynamic of profitability would compel the pursuit of the biggest audiences....

1001. Subscription television is necessarily much the dearest way
of providing a service. If the case for introducing it is to be made out
its supporters have, therefore, to show that the service would bring
marked increases in the range and quality of programming. They
have also to show that these advantages would not be offset by a
decrease in the range and quality of the existing services. In our view,
it is highly unlikely that a service of subscription television would
significantly increase the range and quality of programming. If it
were commercially successful, it would certainly and significantly
reduce the value to viewers of the present service. Some viewers
would, if the service did not have national coverage, be unable to
make this reduction good by paying for the subscription service;
others would not be able to afford to; the rest would pay where now
they do not.... We recommend that no service of subscription television be authorised, whether by wire or ... by radio.

Report of the Committee on Broadcasting 1960 (Chairman: Sir Harry
Pilkington), London: HMSO, Cmd 1753, June 1962, pp. 264, 267.

2.5   The government's response to the
Pilkington Committee report

Two White Papers were published soon after the Committee
published its report. The first (Cmnd 1770, July 1962) was
careful to keep all options open. The second suggested that
further research into the prospects of pay-television was
needed.

45. The Government has considered how far an experiment in pay-
television might help to demonstrate whether or not pay-television is

in the public interest. Before this question can be answered, it is necessary not only to ascertain whether there is likely to be a significant demand for a service, but also to try to measure the impact on BBC and ITA services, the effect on sport and entertainment, and the demand on services generally. It is also necessary to ascertain under conditions of actual operation what rules should govern the conduct of such services, and to test such matters as methods of pricing and programming.

46. The Government takes the view that an experimental arrangement, in pay-television by wire, under controlled conditions – while it could not exclusively demonstrate the long-term effects of pay-television – would give useful information on the public reaction to a service, and would show whether pay-television could find sufficient new programme material to justify itself. The Government has therefore decided to permit such an experimental arrangement.... it would last for some two to three years; there would be no guarantee that on the conclusion of the experiment the Government would authorise a general or permanent pay-television service.

47. The experiment will in any area cater for one pay-television programme only, but wire networks used in the experiment must also make available BBC and ITA programmes ... No advertisements will be allowed....

48. ... In view of the time needed to mount any experiment it is unlikely to start before 1964.

Further Memorandum on the Report of the Committee on Broadcasting 1960, London: HMSO, Cmnd 1893, December 1962, pp. 11–12.

2.6 From pay-television to 'community television': into the 1970s

The Conservative government awarded the third channel to the BBC (see 1.7). That government was replaced by a Labour government in 1964 and it was to remain in power until 1970. For some of that period the field of broadcasting was overseen by Tony Benn. Benn felt that 'the case for pay-TV is a strong one, but the case for a private business monopoly is extremely weak' (1987: 149).

In the mid-1960s, two 'pay-TV' experiments using wires or cables were established in London and in Sheffield. There were only 10,000 subscribers and little prospect of expansion, so the experiments were terminated with the company, Pay-TV Ltd, making losses of around £1 million (see Maddox, 1972: 186–7). The potential rewards for success in this field were so attractive as to encourage others to put forward proposals to exploit the capacity of relay with some form or other of subscription television. But relay operators – by now commonly referred to as cable system operators – felt the need first to establish their community-oriented credentials before going for the rich seam of subscription or pay-television. Backed by Canadian interests, Greenwich Cablevision made the first move.

We ... brought in the two additional channels of Anglia and Southern [Television to the London franchise area] which obviously increased the saleability of the product and expanded the company to virtually its existing size ...

Then again we came up against this saleability problem. It was a political problem to the company as to what it could do next to expand. And of course the Labour Government just tipped out the pay television experiments in Westminster and Sheffield. So that was a non-runner.

But we did examine what was happening in other countries and a local channel originated by the cable company did seem something which was politically viable. And so we were in a position in the September of 1970 to go to Chataway [Christopher Chataway, Minister of Posts and Telecommunications] and put this proposition to him and he immediately liked it ...

... [The idea still] had to be kicked around through all the departments, consultations with the industry, and presumably the Post Office, the BBC and the IBA. And therefore it took us 16 months before we got the announcement of the licence.

D. McEwen, quoted in R. Negrine, 'Cable Television and Community Access', unpublished PhD, University of Leicester, 1978, pp. 158, 169.

2.7 Future technical developments in cable systems: the Television Advisory Committee 1972

Christopher Chataway (the Minister of Posts and Telecommunications) announced the setting up of the community television experiments in the House of Commons in 1972. Following the announcement, experiments were launched in Greenwich, London, and in Swindon (by EMI), Bristol (by Rediffusion), Sheffield (by British Relay) and Wellingborough (by a local group of traders). Although classed by many as failures – the extent of public participation in these services was limited – the public response to these services varied enormously. But with no advertising permitted on these 'experiments' and no possibility of introducing the more lucrative subscription services, the 'community experiments' closed down.

The 'experiments' generated a considerable amount of interest in new ways of providing and producing television; furthermore, their early years coincided with in-depth investigations of the potential of cable systems, just as their later years butted up against the beginnings of the Annan Committee on the Future of Broadcasting.

In 1972 a Television Advisory Committee was set up to explore developments in television, satellite and cable. Though it was fully aware of the range of options available, it made the point that how things developed would 'depend upon the customer demand for additional television and other services, on the cost of providing them, and on political and legal decisions regarding licensing, copyright and other complicated issues' (*Report of the Television Advisory Committee*, p. 66). One of those issues was clearly the cost of providing a national cable infrastructure.

Summary
Distribution by Wire
XIV. The total capital cost of providing a national wired distribution system which would achieve 96 per cent population coverage for six channels is in the order of £500 million. Additional channels could be provided at greater total cost; e.g. a 24 channel network might cost £1,500 million and a project of this size might take 20 years to complete.

XV. Advanced distribution systems are not, before 1985 at the earliest, likely to become so widespread as to provide the possibility of television and sound services additional to those provided by conventional broadcast transmissions....

XVIII. Apart from its normal growth, wired distribution could have a part to play in extending television coverage in remote and rural areas that are difficult to serve. The costs would be very high and it would not generally be profitable. By what agency and on what basis wired distribution should be provided does not fall within our terms of reference.

XIX. Techniques now available could be used to provide local, as distinct from national or regional, programmes – whether by development in existing wired distribution systems or by the provision of new systems.

Ministry of Posts and Telecommunications, *Report of the Television Advisory Committee*, London: HMSO, 1972, pp. 17–19.

2.8   The Annan Committee and cable television

The cost of cabling the entire country, and the time-scale of such a project, was clearly something which could not be entertained easily. Although there was still interest in the development of cable, discussions about broadcasting matters – and policies – in the mid-1970s were affected by a change to a Labour government in 1974 and by the setting up of the Annan Committee on the Future of Broadcasting which acted as a point of focus for all those with an interest in the changing face of British broadcasting. Its report, however, did little to encourage interest in, or the commercial development of, cable.

14.33. ... We do not see cable in the next fifteen years developing as a national service. We consider it will develop as a local community service. Our reasons for thinking so spring from our conception of programming in the United Kingdom and also from technical considerations ... but the programming policy carried most weight with us.

The Future of Cable
14.39. There are many who see cable as the transmission technique of the future, which will vastly extend the number of programmes one can get. The Cable Television Association [CTA] ... want cable services to be developed much more positively in future....

14.40. The CTA envisaged that the proposed [Cable Television] Council would agree with the licensee on the 'package' of programme services provided and the proportion of time to be given to local interest or non-commercial items.... The CTA thought the cable stations would benefit by being able to experiment with providing programmes such as would suit local groups, organisations and traders; local and national bodies concerned with education; those who want programmes on the arts and leisure activities; and those who want to subscribe through Pay TV to see films and sports events. The CTA accepted that, until the market so developed that cable became the primary means of getting one's television service, it would be 'secondary box-office' and Pay TV would be its 'main future at present'. Local television was an important service, but commercially it could not stand on its own feet.

14.41. The CTA did not think that the advent of cable television under the control of an independent authority would adversely affect the quality of television....

14.43. Summing up their evidence, the CTA said that there were four reasons why cable should be given freedom to develop. First, 'because cable has much to offer and it should be given an opportunity to prove its worth'. Secondly, 'because Britain is fortunate in having cable television already available to serve a quarter or more of its homes, which provides a valuable resource from which evolutionary progress can be made'. Thirdly, 'because no progress can be made ... under theoretical conditions or limited experiments'. Fourthly, 'because Britain seems to have a special genius for producing quality in television: it would be a pity if instead of setting her own standards, she had to wait to accept alien standards very different from her own'.

14.44. There was general agreement that cable distribution should be publicly controlled and accountable....

14.45. Some organisations ... thought cable television should develop in the context of an integrated national telecommunications policy....

14.46. Others saw cable developing as a service which disseminated local information, and met local needs....

14.48. ... On cable services there is a simple and strategic choice to be made. Should it develop primarily as a Pay TV or subscription television service ... with a channel available for a local service? Or should it develop primarily as a community resource, a centre which local people can use to make their own programmes?

14.49. ... we do not see cable services being developed as Pay TV.... A cable service can therefore be justified, and attract clients, if it can offer something which the ordinary viewer cannot get off-air.... However, from what we saw in North America we did not conclude that the more channels a viewer could switch to the greater the choice....

14.50. ... we were not persuaded that Pay TV of itself generated new programme material. What it did was to distribute material from broadcasting organisations, feature films and some live sport. It was therefore a ravenous parasite....

14.52. ... if Pay TV were commercially successful, there could well be less choice in the long run for most viewers.... most of us recommend that the cable operators should not be authorised to provide Pay TV services....

14.54. That is why we argue that cable television should develop as a local community service....

25.41. We recommend therefore that, in the 1980s, the relay companies should continue to have a role in local rather than national distribution.... But with the Post Office planning an integrated system, it would be clear from the start that such narrow-band systems would not form part of a national network and would therefore be a relatively short-term high risk investment.....

Report of the Committee on the Future of Broadcasting (Chairman: Lord Annan), London: HMSO, Cmnd 6753, March 1977, pp. 215–22, 395.

2.9 The Callaghan government and cable television, 1978

The 1978 Broadcasting White Paper was less pessimistic about the future of cable than the Annan Committee.

175. ... The Government does not accept that the choice is quite so stark [see 2.8 above]: in principle there seems to be no reason why both pay-television and community cable services should not develop

side by side. It is necessary, therefore, to consider separately the future of community cable services and whether pay-television should be permitted.

Cable as a community resource
176. ... the Government welcomes the [community TV] initiatives which have been taken in this field and hopes that financially viable community cable services can be developed.... these services must satisfy the test of whether the communities in which they operate are prepared to pay for them....

Pay-TV
178. The Government is not prepared at this stage to dismiss the possible advantages of pay-TV, or to conclude that the disadvantages which it might hold could not be overcome.... Provision will therefore be made in the new legislation to enable pilot schemes of Pay-TV to be authorised subject to careful regulation to guard against the possibly damaging effects which pay-TV might have on television as a whole, and on the cinema industry. These safeguards will need to include restrictions on the making of exclusive arrangements for the transmission of sporting events and other events of national significance, and some guarantee that new feature films will be shown first in the cinemas.

Home Office, *Broadcasting*, London: HMSO, Cmnd 7294, 1978, pp. 61–2.

2.10 The Information Technology Advisory Panel

Paradoxically, it was interest in information technology and not interest in cable television *per se* which was to propel it once more on to the agenda. This interest can be traced back to the dying days of the Labour government under James Callaghan and to the interest in information technology which was to feature so prominently under Kenneth Baker, Margaret Thatcher's Minister of Information Technology. Henceforth, cable television became part of the burgeoning information technology revolution.

In 1981, two years after gaining power, Margaret Thatcher

set up the Information Technology Advisory Panel (ITAP) to explore a range of issues related to technological change and communications. The report, published in 1982, effectively broke the seal that had hitherto boxed in the cable industry.

1. Modern cable systems, based on coaxial cables or optical fibres, can provide many new telecommunications-based services to homes and businesses. The initial attraction for home subscribers would be the extra television entertainment channels. However, the main role of cable systems eventually will be the delivery of many information, financial and other services to the home and the joining of businesses and homes by high capacity data links.

2. The United Kingdom currently has cable technology capable of providing economically a wide variety of interactive services, but commercial cable operations, based on the relay of conventional TV broadcasts, are declining and unless firm policy decisions towards cable are taken in 1982, there is a high risk of overseas technological dominance. A further reason for early decision is the possible introduction of direct broadcasting by satellite (DBS) in 1986; if new cable systems can be operating by then, they will provide subscribers with cheaper access to satellite transmissions than is possible with individual aerials, thus improving the market for satellite services, while the DBS programmes will offer an incentive for cable connection. Cable systems and DBS thus complement each other; they are not in opposition.

3. The capital investment required to provide half the United Kingdom population (i.e. those living in urban areas) with modern cable services is of the order of £2,500 million. Subsequent economic activity could be of the order of £1,000 million annually. The consumer electronics industry would benefit greatly, as would optical fibre interests. The indirect effects would include a large stimulus to the office technology industry, whose products would be greatly aided by agreement on cable system standards and the mass production of related components, and for which there are potentially immense world markets.

4. Private sector finance is available for investment in cable systems – there need be no call on public funds. However, it will only be forthcoming if the Government lifts the present constraints on the programmes that may be distributed by cable operation and allows a full range of programmes and services to be provided. Moreover, this

decision must be made quickly to allow prospective operators and investors sufficient time to plan future systems before a change in Government policy can occur. This again points to a decision in 1982.

5. Because the initial attraction of cable systems centres on new channels for broadcast entertainment, news, sport, etc. the implications for current and future broadcasting services have to be considered. Our view is that, while there are dangers which must be guarded against, there are no fundamental reasons for delaying the introduction of new cable services. The regulatory arrangements appropriate for cable systems have, though, to be developed.

6. *Our recommendations are –*

i. The Government should announce as soon as possible its approval for an early start on DBS services.

ii. The Government should announce, by mid-1982, the broad outlines of its future policy towards cable systems, in order to allow the private sector to start planning new systems.

We recommend that the policy should be to license new systems conforming to set technical standards without the present restrictions on programming (apart from obvious requirements on decency, sedition, etc. on which representatives of cable operators have already offered an undertaking). Such licensing could take place initially under existing legislation and administrative arrangements.

iii. The Government should urgently review the implications of cable systems for the financing and regulation of broadcasting and should consider the need for a new statutory body to be the 'broadcasting authority' for cable systems....

2.13 In summary, then, modern cable systems are capable of providing not only a wide range of general TV services, but also specialised services of interest to minority audiences and information and data transfer services unrelated to broadcasting as currently understood. They represent a new form of communication medium. Video cassettes and discs can compete for some types of service, and allow the viewer more freedom in selecting programmes, but cannot provide the same range of services or the same potential for inter-active activities. Satellite transmissions can widen the range of programme material, and can also operate interactively (the telephone system being used to request the services or information required); however, the number of channels available is restricted, with a corresponding constraint on the range of services that can be provided....

8.5 We have ... a paradox. We believe cable to be an essential component of future communications systems, offering great opportunities for new forms of entrepreneurial activity and substantial direct and indirect industrial benefits. However, the initial financing of cable systems will depend upon none of these things, but upon estimates of the revenue from additional popular programming channels. We consider the long term potential of cable systems for providing new sorts of services to be much more important, but have to accept that cable systems will go through an initial phase when their attraction will be based on 'entertainment' considerations. It is, though, essential that the technical specifications set for new cable systems should not preclude the transition from this initial phase to a subsequent phase when cable really does provide a full range of interactive services.

Information Technology Advisory Panel, *Cable Systems*, London: HMSO, 1982, pp. 7–8, 17, 48.

2.11 The Hunt Report on cable systems

Very shortly after the ITAP published its report, the Home Secretary established an inquiry to explore the range of policy options open to the government.

Our task was to consider whether arrangements can now be devised under which cable television and public service broadcasting can coexist without unnecessary inhibitions on the development of the former and without damage to the essentials of the latter.... to provide both positive encouragement to new multi-channel cable operators and at the same time safeguards for public service broadcasting and those who rely on it involves striking a nice balance....

3. Because cable systems will have a *de facto* monopoly, there should be a formal franchising system in which franchises for cable operators should be open to competition.

4. ... the cable operator should be held responsible for the programmes and services he distributes, other than those for which a United Kingdom broadcasting authority takes responsibility....

14. The first source of finance should be the rental charge for a basic package of cable services.

15. Subscription for particular additional services should be

allowed....

18. To enable cable to achieve its full potential, advertising should be permitted....

28. Cable programme services should not be confined to a 'narrowcasting' role. Conversely they should not be subject to the public service broadcasting requirements regarding range and balance....

30. There should be no specific obligations on cable systems to provide facilities for community programming and local access but there should be a presumption that these would be provided and proposals for such facilities should be taken into account in the franchising process.

31. ... Cable programmes (with the exception of specific subscription channels which can be locked by the subscriber) should be subject to the same obligations as the BBC and IBA not to offend good taste and decency ...

46. A new cable authority should be established and given responsibility for awarding franchises and monitoring performance.... The cable authority should be a statutory body....

Report of the Inquiry into Cable Expansion and Broadcasting Policy (Chairman: Lord Hunt of Tamworth), London: HMSO, Cmnd 8679, October 1982, pp. 34–9.

2.12   From the Hunt Report to the White Paper, 1983

The government's 1983 White Paper set out its vision of cable development and the need for a Cable Authority not only to encourage and promote cable's growth but also to regulate it lightly. Thus, 'the Government shares the view of the [Hunt] Inquiry that, once in operation, commercial companies should be free to carry on their business with the minimum of detailed supervision on the part of the Authority' (para. 45). The White Paper also indicated the need to broaden the discussion of cable policy to include discussion of telecommunications policy more generally.

The Cable Authority and a Satellite Broadcasting Board were formally established in 1984 and under the Cable and Broadcasting Act of that year. But the first set of new licences – eleven in all – were issued in 1983 under 'interim' arrangements and pending the appropriate legislation. However, it was the White Paper which set the general pattern for future developments in this field.

214. The Government does not believe that it would be right at this stage in the development of cable to prescribe a particular type of system design....

215. Coaxial cable and optical fibre will be permitted.... the Government does not intend to require the use of optical fibre in any part of a cable system at this stage.

216. The Government wishes to encourage the development of cable systems which will permit the provision both of programme and interactive services....

217. The Government wishes cable investment to be privately financed and market led.... New jobs will be created.... Cable should generate new economic activity and enhance productivity ...

218. A new statutory Cable Authority will be established to award cable franchises and to exercise a measure of oversight over the services provided. The franchising process will stand at the heart of the Authority's activity ...

228. The Government endorses the objective of the BBC and IBA to maintain the range and quality of the broadcasting services now available to all. At the same time the Government accepts that the freedom which it believes it is right to permit for cable development will have implications for the economics of broadcasting. The broadcasters will themselves be free to play a role in cable and they start from a position of strength. In the longer term the growth of cable could necessitate considerable change in existing broadcasting arrangements but cable has first to establish itself and the Government has no plans to modify the existing duties and obligations of the broadcasters....

234. The general and positive programme quality obligations which apply to public service broadcasting will not be appropriate for cable. The Government proposes, however, that all cable channels should be subject to the same good taste and decency rules as existing broadcasting. The Government does not believe that so called 'adult channels' should be available on cable systems....

243. Cable's relationship to the national telecommunications structure has to be considered against the background of the Government's wish to increase competition in the provision of telecommuni-

cation services and apparatus so that industry and the consumer can benefit from resulting improvements in efficiency.

244. The existing national telecommunications operators, BT and Mercury, will not be given the exclusive right to run cable systems nor will their participation in every cable consortium be mandatory. They will however be free to compete with other potential cable providers. In addition:

(1) BT and Mercury will retain the exclusive right both to link local cable systems and to provide voice telephony services on local systems; ...

Home Office and Department of Industry, *The Development of Cable Systems and Services*, London: HMSO, Cmnd 8866, April 1983, pp. 81, 83, 85, 86.

2.13   Setting up the ITAP: Kenneth Baker's view

Kenneth Baker, Minister for Information Technology in 1981 who helped set up the ITAP, described some of the problems the ITAP report brought in its wake.

So here we had an entertainment industry – ITV in cahoots with the BBC, a duopoly – protecting its own privileged positions.... What I saw then was the British genius to institutionalize torpor. I fought back and arranged a seminar in November 1982 at Number 10 with fifty of the top business people from the computing, electronics and communications industries. The Prime Minister was keen, but I had to square the Home Office, which had responsibility for broadcasting and guarded its fiefdom jealously. I soon became convinced that broadcasting policy should not lie with the Home Office, since it was driven by technological change and this was not the Home Office's strong card....

In our Manifesto in 1983 we pledged ourselves to sanction the launch of cable networks to bring choice to consumers not just for entertainment but for the whole range of TV shopping and other interactive services.... A Cable Authority was established and was soon in the process of evaluating bids for franchises. Then came the shuddering halt as a result of Nigel Lawson's first Budget in 1984 when he proposed a major reduction in corporate taxation, accompanied by the removal of capital allowances.... At a stroke, the cabling of Britain came to an end....

K. Baker, *The Turbulent Years: My Life in Politics*, London: Faber and Faber, 1993, pp. 84–5.

2.14 Alternative views on how cable systems should develop

With the Cable Authority in place, further franchises were awarded at fairly regular intervals. But the ITAP/government position on cable, and particularly the calls for liberalisation, had its dissenters. In the end, that opposition failed to alter the course of events, but it does nevertheless illustrate a strong current of opinion then in existence.

4.2 Our opposition focuses first upon the gap to which we have ... drawn attention between the potential and the likely actuality of cable in the real socio-economic context within which it is being introduced. Of course we are in favour in an ideal world of people having more choice of entertainment and wider access to information on an interactive basis. Of course we are in favour of local community services, educational channels, services for the elderly, the disabled, the housebound, services for ethnic minorities. Of course we are in favour of the development of the British electronics industry and of British information technology and related information services and the jobs such development would create. But we see little evidence, and the Government has certainly not produced any, that cable will deliver on such promises.

4.3 The Economics of Cable
The reasons for this are largely economic. Cable is a very expensive distribution medium.... cable is very much in competition with existing broadcasting and telecommunications systems to carry a limited number of services....

This means that the only hope of making profits out of cable is by paring costs to the bone. The first effects of this are being felt on the hardware side with potential systems providers ... buying tried and tested American technology which can be bought off the shelf ...

But the effects of the limited resources available ... are likely to be even more serious on programming. Most potential cable operators are only too ready to admit that there will be no money to pay for either local community or educational programmes.... It is not surprising that the potential cable operators are being coy about any plans they may have about plans for original British production and are arguing that in the early years they couldn't possibly operate if a quota of non EEC material was imposed upon them....

6 Recommendations
... our Councils:-

(a) Should not involve themselves in cable consortia or in the financing of cable systems even were they allowed to do so.

(b) Should not ... provide financing for any cable programming services.

(c) Should concentrate on supporting and developing audio and audio-visual production resources and distribution networks alternative to cable to serve the local community and minorities....

(d) Should ... monitor the existing media and any future cable services, to fight for equality of coverage, access and employment opportunity and for local democratic control of the media.

(e) Should collaborate with other local authorities and ... interested parties ...

1. to ensure that ... franchises are not awarded

2. to ensure that the ... Cable Bill includes the following provisions: ... local authority and trade union representation ..., creation of local cable councils ..., a 14% quota of non EEC material ...

M. Ward and D. Blunkett, *Cable: Report on GLC/Sheffield City Council Hearings on Cable*, July 1983, pp. 13–15, 25–6.

2.15   Cable television versus satellite broadcasting

The rate of cable growth turned out to be much slower than was hoped and instead of small-ish, self-contained, British or European owned systems, the 1990s saw the North American take-over of the British cable industry and the growth of large groupings serving large populations.

One of the reasons for the industry's difficulties was the advent of satellite broadcasting, which seemed to provide much of what cable sought to provide with respect to television but with an immediacy to which cable system operators were not particularly attuned. Hence, the history of the 'new media' in the 1980s is the history of the development of one technology paralleling, and being overtaken by, the development of another.

An early mention of satellite broadcasting can be found in the 1972 Television Advisory Committee report.

Satellite Broadcasting
XI. It is likely that the United Kingdom would be assigned four channels, each capable of accommodating a satellite television service of national coverage on the 625-line standard. Regional variations within each of the four national services would not be possible.

XII. By the time broadcasting from a satellite becomes practicable, improvements in the techniques of transmission (e.g. digital transmission) may have become feasible. Or, improvements in technical standards (e.g. a still higher line definition standard) might be thought desirable. Additional channels afforded by satellite broadcasting could provide an opportunity for adopting such improved techniques or standards.

XIII. Television broadcasting from satellites to the United Kingdom could, if the necessary development work were put in hand, become technically feasible on an experimental basis in the nineteen-eighties; would be confined to the SHF band 11.7–12.5GHz; would need to conform to a frequency plan to be drawn up by an I.T.U. conference which is several years off; and could be expected to provide for four programmes of national or near-national coverage. But the exploitation of satellite broadcasting which cannot start until the nineteen-eighties is unlikely to proceed so far as to provide services to the general public within the duration of the franchise period starting in 1976 and running into the nineteen-eighties.

Ministry of Posts and Telecommunications, *Report of the Television Advisory Committee*, London: HMSO, 1972, p. 18.

2.16   The Annan Committee's view on satellite broadcasting

The Annan Committee's statements on satellite broadcasting run to three paragraphs, or nearly two pages of a 500-page report. The first paragraph referred to the WARC (World

Administrative Radio Conference) agreements as well as to the distinction between satellites for direct home use and for use by broadcast systems (see Negrine, 1988). The second paragraph acknowledged the importance of satellite broadcasting but considered that cable was more flexible. The third paragraph made specific recommendations which the government noted before observing that 'it would be premature to reach any firm conclusions on the allocation of responsibility for satellite transmissions, though it would not wish the IBA to be excluded from any international discussions on this matter' (Cmnd 7294, July 1978, p. 67, para. 203).

25.15. We guess that countries in Western Europe, which have a heavy investment in conventional broadcasting and are relatively small geographically, will not give a high priority to providing broadcasting satellite services. But we cannot rule out the possibility that there will be a move to launch a service in the next 15 years.... We consider it essential that broadcasting satellite services should be licensed and regulated in the same way as the present broadcasting services. Since satellite broadcasting services will provide only national coverage, we recommend that the BBC, as the main instrument of national broadcasting, should carry the responsibilities for the transmission of such services.... we recommend that the BBC should represent the interests of this country. This does not mean, however, that the BBC would necessarily be responsible for production of programmes for satellite channels. Such channels should obviously be used for services of national interest and there could well be scope for European co-operation in programming and transmission....

Report of the Committee on the Future of Broadcasting (Chairman: Lord Annan), London: HMSO, Cmnd 6753, March 1977, p. 385.

2.17   The Home Office report on direct broadcasting by satellite (DBS)

An important study of the options for broadcasting by satellite was produced by the Home Office just prior to the setting up of the ITAP. This study set out the possible lines of development for DBS.

The Nature Of Direct Broadcasting By Satellite

2.1 At a certain distance above the earth's surface (about 36,000 kilometres) the time taken by a satellite to orbit the earth is exactly equal to the time taken for the earth to revolve around its axis (that is, 24 hours). If a satellite is placed in orbit over the equator at that height, it appears, from any point on that part of the earth's surface from which the satellite is visible, to be fixed in the sky. Such a satellite is said to be *geostationary*; the orbit that it describes (*the geostationary orbit*) has the important advantage for broadcasting and telecommunications that the transmitting and receiving equipment do not have to track a moving satellite, and can therefore be less complex. The satellites described in this report as *direct broadcasting satellites* are geostationary satellites....

DBS Coverage

2.10 DBS differs from conventional terrestrial broadcasting in that, broadly speaking, full national coverage can be achieved by a single transmitter on a satellite, whereas a network of transmitters is required to achieve national coverage terrestrially and this network is usually built up over a period of years. A UK DBS service would immediately cover the whole of the United Kingdom and extend to offshore installations which currently cannot receive UK television services. On the other hand a terrestrial transmitter network is more flexible in that it can be planned to permit regional or local variations....

6.41 In broadcasting terms there are arguments in favour of DBS in the opportunities which it would afford for new services; and against DBS in the risks of the new services damaging our existing broadcasting services and resulting in an overall reduction in the quality and range of programmes....

6.42 This analysis suggests a number of conclusions. If the primary aim were to be to minimise the risks to our existing broadcasting services and the new services which are to be introduced over the next few years, probably no start with DBS at all, and certainly no early start in the mid-1980s, would seem preferable. No start at all, however, carries other risks of its own. It would mean that the UK had decided to opt out of a development which other industrial countries, including our European neighbours, are experimenting with and one which could prove important; and because there is a long lead time in introducing DBS services it could be difficult to retrieve the position quickly if the decision not to introduce DBS were to prove mistaken. If DBS were to be successful in Europe but the UK had opted out, the UK might itself become increasingly cut off from an important element of European cultural and technological development; and despite the difficulties discussed ..., viewers might turn increasingly to the European services which grew and prospered at the expense of our own.

Home Office, *Direct Broadcasting By Satellite*, London: HMSO, May 1981, pp. 5, 6, 40.

2.18   The ITAP's view of satellite broadcasting

The ITAP was also aware of the possible uses of satellite broadcasting – and not in the very distant future. This influenced its thinking about the need for 'early' decisions on cable, and its general view of the relationship between these two developing means of communication.

2. The United Kingdom currently has cable technology capable of providing economically a wide variety of interactive services, but commercial cable operations, based on the relay of conventional TV broadcasts, are declining and unless firm policy decisions towards cable are taken in 1982, there is a high risk of overseas technological dominance. A further reason for early decision is the possible introduction of direct broadcasting by satellite (DBS) in 1986; if new cable systems can be operating by then, they will provide subscribers with cheaper access to satellite transmissions than is possible with individual aerials, thus improving the market for satellite services, while the DBS programmes will offer an incentive for cable connection. Cable systems and DBS thus complement each other; they are not in opposition....

4.1 The response of commercial interests to the Home Office report on DBS ... has, we understand, been very positive. There has been strong support for the 'modest early start' option put forward in the report and there seems a good chance of a two-channel UK satellite broadcasting service commencing in 1986. Private sector finance for the necessary satellite appears to be forthcoming and the BBC and other organisations wish to lease channels and offer programmes.

Current BBC plans include one channel of 'the best of BBC1 and BBC2' and a second, subscription TV channel showing predominantly feature films. Market research by the BBC has shown that perhaps 10 per cent of households would install individual DBS receivers by 1990....

4.14 Our conclusions on the relationship between the introduction of United Kingdom DBS services and cable systems are, therefore –

i. There is no need to regard DBS and cable as alternatives or opponents, rather they complement each other. Existing cable systems, assuming they are still operating in 1986, can provide DBS with a substantial audience. New systems could enable many subscribers to receive DBS programmes at a lower cost than individual reception, while the DBS programmes would help to attract subscribers. And for an unknown number of people, particularly in urban areas, cable may be the only practicable means of receiving DBS transmissions.

ii. No decisions on cable affect any of the planning for DBS....

iii. Without policy decisions in a timescale much faster than at present envisaged new systems cannot be installed in time to distribute DBS transmissions from the start, and the growth of both cable and DBS subscribers will be correspondingly inhibited. Moreover, without such decisions, many existing cable services will have ceased operation by 1986.

iv. Once DBS services are well established ... it will be increasingly difficult for new cable systems to be established....

v. The Government's future policy towards cable systems needs therefore to be developed and announced by the middle of 1982 if cable is to offer DBS significant support from the start. If this timescale is not met, not only will many existing commercial cable systems cease to function, but the viability of DBS could be prejudiced.

Information Technology Advisory Panel, *Cable Systems*, London: HMSO, 1982, pp. 7, 22, 26–7.

2.19   DBS, the BBC and the IBA

Following the publication of the Home Office study in 1981, the BBC was awarded the licence to run DBS in the UK, with a proposed starting date in 1986. This decision ensured that the existing structure, and quality, of British programming would continue through yet another means of communication. Unfortunately, the details of the licence created their own problems: there were conditions pertaining to the nature of the satellite system and who should build it, the transmission system to be used, and the source of funds.

The BBC eventually abandoned its plans for DBS but the IBA took up the challenge and set out its own plans for DBS services, alongside its own specifications for this new venture, a venture which was to become British Satellite Broadcasting (BSB) in 1986.

1.1 The Home Secretary has brought into force Sections 37–41 of the Cable and Broadcasting Act 1984 ('the 1984 Act') which give powers to the Independent Broadcasting Authority to provide television and teletext services by means of direct broadcasting by satellite ('DBS'). Under international agreement, five DBS channels have been allocated to the United Kingdom. Initially three of these channels will be available to the IBA. The Home Secretary has announced that broadcasting on the two remaining channels shall not begin until the new service has been in operation for at least three years.

1.2 The IBA is now inviting applications for the provision of DBS programme services.... the IBA will be the broadcaster of the services. ... the IBA will be responsible for appointing a programme contractor or contractors, for overseeing the programming and controlling advertisements, and for the transmission of the services. With regard to transmission, the IBA will be responsible for the up-link to the satellite....

1.3 In announcing his decision to bring into force the relevant sections of the 1984 Act, the Home Secretary stated that, as to the source of satellite provision, it would be open to potential contractors to consider proposals from suppliers either in the United Kingdom or overseas. He envisaged that, in assessing applications, the IBA would take account of the overall economic implications for the UK. Applicants will accordingly be asked to state what economic benefits they believe their proposals will bring to the UK....

TRANSMISSION STANDARD
2.4 The Government's announced policy is that the transmission standard for UK DBS services should be C-MAC. The IBA fully supports this choice of standard, which it believes has significant

technical and commercial advantages....

PROGRAMMING
2.6 Under the terms of the 1981 and 1984 Acts, all the IBA's services
are required to be of high quality (both as to the transmission and as
to the matter transmitted). The IBA's DBS services are not required to
maintain a wide range of subject matter. A DBS channel could therefore consist largely of one type of programming....
2.9 ... With regards to the requirement for proper proportions of
British/EEC programming, the IBA will place emphasis on the need
for British/EEC programming to be included in the service: but no
fixed British/EEC quota will be laid down in advance....

Independent Broadcasting Authority, *DBS Contract Specification
Document IBA DBS 1, Programme Contract Specification*, London: IBA,
1986, pp. 1, 5, 6.

2.20 BSB and the regulator

BSB was awarded the contract to provide DBS services. The
BSB consortium included Granada, Pearson, Virgin, and
Anglia Television. Following the specifications set out by the
IBA, it went for an appropriate – and costly – high-power
satellite and the required (albeit untried) transmission system. The intention was to launch in 1989. What was always a
risky venture became even riskier when it emerged that
satellite systems were to be launched through organisations
based in Luxemburg, and that those systems would be able to
transmit to the UK. Though not licensed by the IBA as DBS,
these systems would provide competition for BSB.

43.–(2) ... 'non-domestic satellite service' means –
(a) a service ... by satellite –
(i) otherwise than on an allocated frequency, and
(ii) for general reception in the United Kingdom ...
where the programmes are transmitted from a place in the United
Kingdom; or
(b) a service ... by satellite –
(i) from a place which is neither in the United Kingdom nor in any
prescribed country, but

(ii) [for reception in the United Kingdom] ... and provided by a person in the United Kingdom....

45.– (1) An application for a licence to provide a non-domestic satellite service shall –

(a) be made in such manner as the Commission may determine; and

(b) be accompanied by such fee (if any) as they may determine.

(2) ... the Commission ... may only refuse to grant the licence applied for if it appears to them that the services ... would not comply with the requirements [relating to 'taste and decency', etc.].

Broadcasting Act 1990, pp. 43–4.

2.21 Regulating satellite services

The launch of the Astra satellite, a sixteen-channel satellite, in June 1988 with Rupert Murdoch's Sky Television on board changed the whole satellite broadcasting scene at a stroke. Though initially seen as a gamble and a gamble which later threatened the survival of the whole organisation, it was a gamble which paid off. Sky Television also pounced on BSB.

Although the ITC had responsibility over domestic satellite services, the limits of its authority became clear at the end of 1990 when Rupert Murdoch's Sky Television took over BSB. Technically, the merger breached the cross-ownership regulations contained in the Broadcasting Act 1990. David Mellor, the Arts Minister, told a conference on broadcasting, 'These are commercial activities and however much we in Parliament like to think we call the shots we don't: the market calls the shots' (*The Guardian*, 6 November 1990). In the event, the government cleared the merger and decided not to refer it to the Monopolies and Mergers Commission; Rupert Murdoch ended up with a 50 per cent, later 40 per cent, stake in BSkyB.

By the end of 1997, Murdoch's BSkyB had bought up exclusive rights to televise on his subscription services football, rugby union, golf, rugby league, boxing, cricket and other events. One could argue that this impoverished terrestrial broadcasting systems – they could not afford what BSkyB offered – and endangered the whole nation's possible enjoyment of sporting fixtures which had hitherto been free.

British Satellite Broadcasting's contract for five channels of satellite television is to be terminated by the Independent Broadcasting Authority as a result of BSB's merger with Sky Television. The IBA said the contract would not be withdrawn immediately, 'in the interest of viewers'. It will consider reallocating BSB's franchise, and has asked for fresh proposals for provision of television services on BSB's frequencies.

In its first full statement on the merger, agreed in secret by BSB's shareholders and Rupert Murdoch's Sky Television two weeks ago, the IBA said it considered the merger 'for which the IBA's consent was neither obtained nor sought' a serious breach of BSB's contract.

It is understood that there were differences of opinion among members of the authority some of whom wanted to withdraw BSB's franchise immediately but it was decided that it would be unfair to the 120,000 people who had bought BSB 'squarials' to deprive them of programmes before they could get Astra equipment....

The IBA statement also leaves a question mark over future licensing arrangements for BSkyB. Under the 1990 Broadcasting Act non-domestic satellite services such as Sky, and now BSkyB, need to get a licence from the Independent Television Commission, which takes over from the IBA in January. The IBA is taking further legal advice on whether the breach of contract by BSB's shareholders means that the new company would not be a 'fit and proper' holder of any television licence, which would throw into question the continuation of BSkyB even on the Astra system....

'IBA to pull the plug on BSB contract', *The Guardian*, 17 November 1990, p. 4.

2.22 The competitive 'new' media environment: satellite, cable and telecommunications

Satellite broadcasting undermined cable. The 'hand in hand' approach which was a feature of talk in the 1980s gave way to competition as satellite dishes began to proliferate. Cable companies continued to argue that they could offer what satellite broadcasting did and more, e.g. telephony and interactivity, even when the spotlight shifted to digital broadcasting. But the absence of a concerted marketing strategy left

cable systems at the starting blocks while satellite broadcasting continued to prosper.

There was another potential threat to cable companies.
British Telecom (BT), which began to move into private ownership from 1982 onwards, also wished to offer entertainment services on its network. The policy of the Conservative
government prohibited that possibility, but only until the turn
of the century (option 2.12 below).

1.2 In November 1983 the Government announced that it did not
intend to license operators other than British Telecommunications plc
and Mercury Communications Ltd (Mercury) to provide the basic
telecommunications service of conveying messages over fixed links,
whether cable, radio or satellite, both domestically and internationally, during the following seven years. This was to give Mercury time
to install and consolidate its network and to enable BT to adjust to
competition. The Government said that the position would then be
reviewed.... The policy of licensing only BT and Mercury to provide a
service over fixed links subsequently became known as the duopoly
policy.

1.3 In its July 1986 report of *Financing the BBC* (Cmnd 9824), the
Peacock Committee recommended that national telecommunication
systems (ie BT, Mercury and any subsequent entrants) should be permitted to act as common carriers.... In its November 1988 Broadcasting White Paper (Cm 517), the Government said that, while it saw the
attraction in the underlying idea as a route to additional competition
in the entertainment services market, implementation of the recommendation in its original form would be impracticable and could in-
hibit the growth of competition in telecommunications networks. The
Government therefore concluded that it would examine the recommendation further at the time the duopoly policy was reviewed....

2.4 The Director General [of Telecommunications] has indicated
that, in the light of market developments since the terms of the standard cable franchise licences were settled, he doubts the need for him
to make a determination before cable operators can offer voice
telephony services. He is therefore inclined to offer each cable operator the option of being released from this requirement ...

2.11 ... [The Government] proposes not to remove the present
restrictions in telecommunications operators' licences unless and
until they are allowed to *provide* entertainment services, but it would

The end of scarcity

welcome comments on whether any new operators should be allowed
to *convey* both entertainment and telecommunications services.

2.12 The Government is inclined:

(a) to make a commitment at the completion of the present review
that it intends, ten years from that date, to allow BT and other
national public telecommunications operators to *provide* entertainment services nationally over their main networks;

(b) to be prepared to reconsider this commitment after seven years
...;

(c) to leave to be decided nearer the time the terms and conditions
on which national public telecommunications operators would be
allowed to provide entertainment services; and

(d) in the meantime, to allow the parents, subsidiaries and associates of national public telecommunications operators, but not such
operators themselves, to tender for any local delivery franchise advertised ...

Department of Trade and Industry, *Competition and Choice: Telecommunications Policy for the 1990s, A Consultative Document*, London:
HMSO, Cm 1303, November 1990, pp. 1, 4, 5–6.

2.23   The return of the 'wired nation'

With one set of competitors in check, cable systems were still
bearing the brunt of competition from BSkyB. One attempt to
revive interest in the cable industry was contained in a parliamentary Trade and Industry Select Committee report, *Optical Fibre Networks*.

2. The potential now exists for an enormous range of new services,
which are likely to have profound consequences for economic performance and for the ways in which people organise their business
and social lives. The Government has a significant role in this area,
especially through the way it regulates the relevant industries. *There
is concern that government policies could be hindering or not sufficiently encouraging the development of the most advanced infrastructure and services, and that this could result in the UK falling behind
other countries, with damaging consequence.* This concern was the
reason for our inquiry....

85

The role of Government

21. Virtually none of our witnesses suggested that the Government should be directly involved in providing infrastructure.... The principal role of governments is to provide an appropriate regulatory system, but other aspects include support of research and development, promoting the development of broadband services, particularly where the government's own services can benefit, and defining and ensuring the implementation of a universal service obligation....

23. The government's telecommunications policy has been based on the principle of increasing competition in the supply of both infrastructure and services....

24. ... The main feature of the White Paper (1990) was the Government's intention to end the duopoly. In order to increase competition at both local and national levels, operators other than BT and Mercury, including the cable television companies, were to be allowed to provide telecommunications services in their own right, rather than as agents of BT or Mercury. The cable companies were to be allowed not only to provide both entertainment and telephony [something which BT is not allowed to do], but also to connect their systems with each other.

25. Thus Government policies have had two main objectives: to promote competition in telecommunications and to facilitate the establishment of cable television networks. The policies have not been designed to promote the development of broadband networks and services, at least since the change in policy towards cable networks in 1988 ...

64. ... *we recommend that the Government and OFTEL actively seek to promote the highest technical standards and the greatest possible technical compatibility between the networks....*

77. ... *we recommend that the Government and OFTEL examine the possibility of encouraging PTOs [public telecommunications operators] and cable companies to co-operate in providing broadband infrastructure in areas where there is no likelihood of cable television franchises being awarded by the end of 1995....*

85. ... *We believe that an early lifting of the restrictions [on BT] would be likely to promote investment in broadband infrastructure by BT and perhaps other national PTOs, possibly on a large scale....*

108. ... *We ... recommend that the Government make clear that all restrictions on PTOs conveying or providing entertainment will be lifted by the end of 2002, providing that PTOs permit fair and open*

access to their networks....

113. ... *We recommend that the Government adopt a more active and co-ordinated approach to the development of broadband applications for the public sector....*

125. ... *We urge the Government to continue to press for liberalisation of telecommunications markets in the US, the EU and elsewhere....*

127. ... *we recommend that the Government review the structure of telecommunications and broadcasting regulation in order to ensure consistent principles and clear responsibilities in all matters relevant to broadband regulation and development....*

132. Although it will be the private sector which builds the networks and provides the services, the Government has several major roles. While we agree with many of the general principles the Government is following, we have three general criticisms:

– government policy is too concerned with infrastructure and competition in existing services and needs to be refocused on broadband services;

– there appears to be little sense of urgency, as shown by its attitude to the restrictions on PTOs;

– there is a lack of clear sense of vision or excitement about what broadband communications could do for the UK and its people; in short, there is a lack of the type of leadership being shown in the US.

Trade and Industry Committee, *Optical Fibre Networks*, Third Report, 19 July 1994, London: HMSO, Session 1993–94, HCP 285-I, pp. 9, 14, 16, 28–9, 32, 34, 41, 42, 45, 46, 47.

2.24 From the 'wired society' to 'information superhighways'

In 1995 the Parliamentary Office of Science and Technology produced a report which reviewed the nature of past policies in respect of telecommunications and, at the same time, outlined the possible changes in technologies and policies which could take place in the future, if only to encourage 'wealth creation'.

The current debate on the NII [National Information Infrastructure or National Superhighway] contains some echoes of the earlier concept of a 'wired' society triggered in the early 1980s by the availability of optical fibres....

... what really distinguishes the current debate on the 'superhighway' from the earlier concept of the wired society is the extent to which several fields have 'converged' in a technological sense, to make possible at relatively low cost a whole range of applications of computing and telecommunications which could only have been imagined ten years ago. Then, various technologies were split into those which were digital ..., and the field of entertainment and other sources of information which were 'analogue' in nature. In the last few years however, these two separate paths are converging rapidly and soon the telecommunications, computing, broadcast, entertainment and information businesses will be inextricably linked by common digital technology....

... The outcome of all these [technological] developments is that it is no longer a simple question of whether or not to have a single optical fibre-based infrastructure, as in the original concept of the wired society. The concept of a national information infrastructure is much more how the various parts of the existing infrastructure can be encouraged to work together to greatest effect and develop in the most synergistic manner. This means that the current debate is much more complex than the simple wired society debate of ten years ago, and presents even greater challenges for public policy development....

The Government response [to the DTI report] in November 1994 reiterated its commitment to encouraging competition in telecoms and did not accept the committee's main recommendation to set a firm date for lifting restrictions on BT and Mercury, concluding that the existing regulatory framework (as expressed in the 1991 Telecommunications White Paper) continued to provide the best framework for developing internationally competitive telecommunications in the UK. The emphasis on stability of the regulatory framework led the government to reject calls for restrictions to be removed in 2002 ...

Some argue that in view of the plethora of technologies involved and the unpredictability of their relative future roles, there is very little role for public policy in attempting to influence the way in which the NII develops. Others disagree, and argue that public policy has a role in many areas to maximise economic and social benefits, while attempting to guard against negative social impacts....

Parliamentary Office of Science and Technology, *Information 'Super-highways': The UK National Information Infrastructure*, London: HMSO, May 1995, pp. 2, 3, 4, 15, 102.

2.25   The Labour Party and the NII

Whilst in opposition, the Labour Party began to develop its own set of policies towards the NII. In 1995 it published *Communicating Britain's Future*. This contained something of its vision for the future.

Labour came to power after the May 1997 general election. At the time of writing (Spring 1998), specific policy documents on the duopoly review had not yet been produced.

We believe that the physical infrastructure of the new communications networks will and must be developed by the private sector. The competitive and regulatory environment will therefore be crucial in influencing how it evolves....

Our fundamental aim must be to see a truly nationwide network developed, as rapidly as possible.... We envisage a variety of different providers of infrastructure, in competition in some areas and standing alone in others. British Telecom, the cable television companies, and other telephony providers, should all be able to compete....

We believe there is a strong case for ending the uncertainty currently affecting BT and other telephony providers, and making explicit the timetable for them to enter the entertainment market. *We conclude that the proposal advanced by the Trade and Industry Select Committee, for a rolling programme of entry into the cable franchise areas beginning in 1998, is the best basis to achieve this. We believe that this would protect the legitimate interests of the cable companies themselves, while providing certainty for BT and others, and ensuring a proper competitive environment for the benefit of the consumer. We would also propose ... that full and open competition be permitted everywhere from 2002.*

In return for ending the present uncertainty for telephony operators, we would expect a commitment from them to a specific timetable of provision. *In particular, we would require from BT and others that they establish a clear programme of provision of broadband communication links that will ensure, over time, that the whole country – as far as is practicable – is reached....*

   ... we believe it is important to ensure that the new networks are not just mechanisms for improving business to business communication, important though that objective is. Nor should they just be about the delivery of more and better targetted home entertainment. It is also vital that we seek the best possible social uses for the new interactive technologies. *To this end, we shall insist that the providers of the networks lay a two-way broadband feed into every public library, every school, every health centre, every hospital and every Citizen's Advice Bureau.*

Labour Party, *Communicating Britain's Future*, London: Labour Party, 1995, pp. 7, 17.

3

Broadcasting and political communication

In the period immediately after the Second World War, the BBC television service was very much still in its infancy. Radio was the dominant medium. But from the beginnings of the 1950s, television began to challenge the dominance of radio. Events such as the televising of the Coronation in 1953 confirmed the significance of television for the nation as a whole.

In the world of politics, though, television in the early 1950s was regarded with considerable suspicion. So much so that it was bound by a number of restrictions, such as those contained in the *Aide Mémoire*, which severely limited what it could and could not do. This situation lasted roughly until the second half of the 1950s when broadcasters began to develop their own ways of coping with political content. It was in this period that the 14-Day Rule was abandoned (1956/57), that election coverage began to develop (1958), that Independent Television and Independent Television News became established (1955/56), and that the first major domestic political interview took place (1958). All these points mark the beginnings of a transition which has often been caricatured as from one of deference to political actors to a more questioning stance.

It would be wrong, though, to think of the transition in terms of broadcasting alone. Other media and other factors also impinged on how broadcasters began to adapt their practices to the needs of political actors, and vice versa. Similarly, it is important to consider the four areas discussed here – the removal of restrictions on political broadcasting in the 1950s, the changing nature of election coverage, the introduction of television into the House of Commons, and the moments of crisis in the relationship between broadcasters and politicians – not as distinct areas but as overlapping areas in as much as changing practices in one contributed to changes in others.

THE REMOVAL OF RESTRICTIONS ON
POLITICAL BROADCASTING

3.1 The 14-Day Rule

The 14-Day Rule reflected a concern about the proper relationship between broadcasting and Parliament. Was there a
danger that broadcasting would divert attention away from
Parliament and usurp its authority? That concern was graphi-
cally expressed by Winston Churchill, when Prime Minister,
in a now often-quoted extract. His view was often echoed by
MPs in countless debates about the televising of the Commons (see below), even though it was not a universally shared
view.

In accordance with the practice, which has existed by agreement
between the BBC and the major political parties for a number of
years, the BBC avoids broadcasting discussions on an issue when it is
to be debated in Parliament within a fortnight [the '14-Day Rule'].
Her Majesty's Government is therefore prepared to give what information it can if inquiries are made by the BBC about the likelihood of
a debate on a particular subject....

Mr Grimond: Will not the Prime Minister reconsider this matter?
Could it not be left to the good sense of the BBC to exercise its discretion?

The Prime Minister: No, Sir. I will never reconsider it. It would be
shocking to have debates in this House forestalled time after time by
expressions of opinion by persons who had not the status or responsibility of Members of Parliament....

... I have always attached great importance to Parliament and to
the House of Commons. I am quite sure that the bringing on of exciting debates in these vast, new robot organisations of television and
BBC broadcasting to take place before a debate in this House, might
have deleterious effects upon our general interests, and that honour-
able Members should be considering the interests of the House of
Commons, to whom we all owe a lot.

Winston Churchill, *House of Commons Debates*, 23 February 1955,
vol. 537, cols 1276–7.

3.2   The history of the '14-Day Rule'

The wartime origins of the rule reveal the BBC as an organisation which was unsure of its political role and saw itself as
subservient to the political parties. It was also uncertain
about how to deal with its political masters.

'THE FORTNIGHT RULE': A CHRONOLOGICAL SUMMARY,
1944–55
Wartime Origins
1. 10th February, 1944. The Board of Governors considered the situation which has arisen as a result of the authorisation by the Minister
of Information of a talk ... by the President of the Board of Education
on the eve of the Second Reading of the Education Bill then before
Parliament. The Governors passed a resolution in the following
terms:
RESOLVED that when a debate on a major matter of public policy
is imminent or is actually taking place in Parliament, the BBC cannot
allow the broadcasting of Ministerial or other *ex parte* statements
thereon. This rule shall not apply to matters directly affecting the war
effort, or in circumstances of national emergency.
In subsequent practice the word 'imminent' was variously construed as from a fortnight to a month.
2. The 'Fortnight Rule', as it later came to be known, was thus self-
imposed by the BBC in the form of a Governors' resolution. Although
the object at the time was to prevent any recurrence of a situation in
which a Ministerial broadcast had been imposed on the BBC at a time
when the issue dealt with in the broadcast was before Parliament, the
inclusion in the Resolution of the words 'or other *ex parte* statements
thereon' had the effect of excluding also any such broadcasts on the
subject which the BBC might otherwise have wished to put out as part
of its normal programme.
3. November, 1945. After the war, the BBC consulted with the parliamentary leaders with a view to the resumption of political broadcasting on lines to be agreed. As a result, the BBC sent to the Lord
Privy Seal ... a draft agreement containing the following proposal,
among others:
When a debate on a major matter of policy is imminent or actually
taking place in Parliament, the BBC should not allow broadcasts of
Ministerial or other *ex parte* statements thereon until the Bill has had

its Third Reading in the House ... or the business has been completed.

January, 1946. In his reply, Mr. Greenwood said:

The Government do not think it desirable to attempt to reduce to written rules the principles which should govern the BBC in regard to political broadcasting.

The principles to be adopted must depend on good sense and good will ...

Mr Greenwood proposed instead 'a few short principles' which should be 'regarded as a mere aide mémoire'....

8. February, 1947. On 25th February, 1947, the Prime Minister (Mr. Attlee) forwarded to the BBC a printed copy of the *Aide Mémoire*, paragraph 6(iv) of which reads:

No broadcasts arranged by the BBC other than the normal reporting of parliamentary proceedings are to take place on any question while it is the subject of discussion in either House.

9. A feature of the *Aide Mémoire* is that it settled the question of Ministerial broadcasts [see below]. By introducing safeguards against Ministerial broadcasts of a controversial character, the *Aide Mémoire* removed the danger from which the BBC had sought to defend itself by means of its own Fortnight Rule.

BBC Memorandum 1, 'The Fortnight Rule', 7 March 1956, in *Report of the Select Committee on Broadcasting (Anticipation of Debates)*, 17 May 1956, London: HMSO, Session 1955–56, HC 288, pp. 23–5.

3.3 The *Aide Mémoire*

The *Aide-Mémoire* of 6 February 1947 was revised in July 1948. The revisions contained the restrictions which related to reporting of matters which arose in Parliament (Clause 6(iv)), as well as more general guidelines in respect of controversial broadcasting, for example party political broadcasts. The *Aide Mémoire* related to both radio and television.

1. It is desirable that political broadcasts of a controversial nature shall be resumed.

2. In view of their responsibilities for the care of the nation the government should be able to use the wireless from time to time for ministerial broadcasts which, for example, are purely factual, or

explanatory of legislation or administrative policies approved by parliament; or in the nature of appeals to the nation to co-operate in national policies, such as fuel economy or recruiting, which require the active participation of the public. Broadcasts on state occasions also come in the same category.

It will be incumbent on ministers making such broadcasts to be as impartial as possible, and in the ordinary way there will be no question of a reply by the opposition. Where, however, the opposition think that a government broadcast is controversial it will be open to them to take the matter up through the usual channels with a view to a reply.

i As a reply if one is to be made should normally be within a very short period after the original broadcast, say three days, the BBC will be free to exercise its own judgement if no agreement is arrived at within that period....

3. 'Outside' broadcasts, e.g. of speeches at party conferences which are in the nature of news items, shall carry no right of reply by the other side.

4. A limited number of controversial party political broadcasts shall be allocated to the various parties in accordance with their polls at the last general election....

6.(ii) The BBC reserve the right, after consultation with the party leaders, to invite to the microphone a member of either House of outstanding national eminence who may have become detached from any party.

(iii) Apart from these limited broadcasts on major policy the BBC are free to invite members of either House to take part in controversial broadcasts of a round-table character in which political questions are dealt with, provided two or more persons representing different sides take part in the broadcasts.

(iv) No broadcasts arranged by the BBC other than the normal reporting of parliamentary proceedings are to take place on any question while it is the subject of discussion in either House.

[The revisions in July 1948 related to clause 6(iv) which would now] be construed as:

(a) that the BBC will not have discussions or *ex parte* statements on any issues for a period of a fortnight before they are debated in either House;

(b) that while matters are subjects of legislation MPs will not be used in such discussions.

BBC Memorandum 8, in *Report of the Committee on Broadcasting 1949* (Chairman: Lord Beveridge), London: HMSO, Cmd 8116, January 1951, Appendix H, pp. 109–10.

3.4   The Broadcasting Committee 1949 and 'controversial broadcasting'

The 1949 Broadcasting Committee was aware of the difficulties faced by the BBC in attempting to reflect all shades of political opinion and to offer insights into the political process. The BBC wanted looser interpretations than were used in the *Aide Mémoire* so that 'while the BBC took care not to become a simultaneous alternative debating arena to Parliament, it should be free in discussions and other broadcasts reasonably to deal with matters which ... were of outstanding public interest' (BBC Memorandum 1, p. 24).

The BBC's representations to the Committee produced little change, though the 1949 Committee acknowledged the problems and was also greatly concerned that the BBC should continue to act in such a way as to enhance democratic life.

259. The treatment of political issues in broadcasting raises several important and interesting issues. Clearly, where the total number of independent broadcasting authorities is strictly limited by physical conditions ... the authorities themselves cannot be allowed to be political partisans.... to bar all political controversy from the microphone would be to waste an invaluable means of securing the discussion which is the essence of democracy.... [Allowing broadcasters to deal in controversies is] a necessary step in drawing from the new instrument of communication its maximum of service to the community. More than this, it is essential that the broadcasting authority, in allotting opportunity for ventilation of controversial views, should not be guided either by simple calculation of the numbers who already hold such views, or by fear of giving offence to particular groups of listeners. Minorities must have the chance by persuasion of turning themselves into majorities.

260. Our impression is that in general the problem of allowing a fair field of controversy and for minorities has been handled in this country with a considerable measure of success. We doubt whether a multiplicity of broadcasting authorities would be an advantage for

this particular purpose....

261. ... there cannot be a continuous balancing night by night or week by week of everything that is said on the microphone. All that can be asked of the BBC is both that there should be no bias in the allocation of facilities over a substantial period, and that the method of organisation of controversial talks should be such as to make it plain that there can be no bias....

264. ... an early opportunity should be taken of reconsidering [the 14-Day Rule].... simultaneous broadcasting of the Parliamentary Debates themselves could hardly fail to influence the character of the debates in a way which most people in Britain would think harmful. But we do not see why the British democracy should not be allowed to have microphone debate of a political issue at the time when a debate is most topical and interesting, that is to say when the issue is actually before Parliament. This would both increase popular interest in Parliament and popular capacity to judge the wisdom of Parliament. Both these things are gains from the point of view of good democratic government.

Report of the Committee on Broadcasting 1949 (Chairman: Lord Beveridge), London: HMSO, Cmd 8116, January 1951, pp. 66–9.

3.5 The imposition of restrictions on the BBC

By 1954, there was still no change to the Rule (see 3.1). Grace Wyndham Goldie, one of the BBC's first producers of televised political programmes, believed that the Rule was never meant to be a binding agreement, contrary to the views of the political parties of the day. The BBC thus took the view that it need not accept the restrictions unless they were laid down in its Charter and Licence and so it decided that it should use its own discretion with regard to broadcast discussions about political matters which might be debated in Parliament. The government's response was a prescriptive directive, dated 27 July 1955.

To the British Broadcasting Corporation.

1. In accordance with Clause 15 (4) of the Corporation's licence and agreement dated 12th June, 1952, I hereby require:

(a) that the Corporation shall not, on any issue arrange discussions or ex-parte statements which are to be broadcast during a period of a fortnight before the issue is debated in either House or while it is being so debated;

(b) that when legislation is introduced in Parliament on any subject, the Corporation shall not, on such subject, arrange broadcasts by any Member of Parliament which are to be made during the period between the introduction of the legislation and the time when it either receives the Royal Assent or is previously withdrawn or dropped.

2. These requirements do not affect the normal reporting of Parliamentary proceedings in accordance with Clause 15 (2) of the licence and agreement.

BBC Memorandum 1, 'The Fortnight Rule', 7 March 1956, in *Report of the Select Committee on Broadcasting (Anticipation of Debates)*, 17 May 1956, London: HMSO, Session 1955–56, HCP 288, p. 28. See also G. W. Goldie, *Facing the Nation: Television and Politics, 1936–1976*, London: The Bodley Head, 1977, p. 125.

3.6 From 'agreement' to 'prescription'

Whilst the agreement was in place, the BBC interpreted the 14-Day Rule in a flexible way, and in such a way that political discussion on-air was possible. Once the prescription was produced, the room for flexibility was much more limited.

2. The BBC not only decides the occasions on which the rule must be applied but also what it is that must be excluded. The earliest form of the rule ... left a wide scope for interpretation ... In practice the BBC applied the rule only in cases of a major debate in either House; it first construed the word 'imminent' variously as being a fortnight or a month.

3. Later, more exact formulations of the rule brought with them more exact observance.... in 1948 when the programme 'Any Questions?' was started, the BBC did not consider that this programme was within the scope of what was intended by the Agreement. The spontaneous nature of this and other question and answer programmes led the BBC to feel that this type of programme was not thought to be the object of the restriction.... No account was taken of Private Members' Bills and MPs were permitted to discuss matters

connected with Government legislation until the Second Reading debates drew near.

4. The maximum application of the rule in detail has been felt only since the agreement gave place to the prescription.... For example, the programme 'Any Questions?' ... seems clearly to fall within the terms of the prescription and is therefore now subject to the rule whereas previously it was largely unaffected.

BBC Memorandum 2, 'The Fortnight Rule', 7 March 1956, in *Report of the Select Committee on Broadcasting (Anticipation of Debates)*, 17 May 1956, London: HMSO, Session 1955–56, HC 288, p. 30.

3.7   Changes in the context of the communication of politics

> Though the 14-Day Rule did create problems for broadcast-
> ers and it did prevent them from making topical programmes,
> the BBC was still able to operate within the confines of that
> rule and to make contributions to political debate. Grace
> Wyndham Goldie gives several examples of programmes in
> the early 1950s, such as *In the News*, which sought to give
> space to politicians to discuss issues of public interest. Such
> programmes, however, were more 'current affairs' than news
> at a time when 'newsreels' were more the order of the day and
> news programmes *per se* had not yet developed as a genre.

When, on July 5, 1954, 'News and Newsreel' at last appeared on the screen it was pretentious, unattractive and lamentably amateurish.... It started with a pompous display of the BBC's coat of arms. This was followed by a series of printed captions, like paragraph headings in a newspaper. These were laid in vision while an announcer, out of vision, read the appropriate item of news.

... The trouble was not only that the News Division ... was inexperienced in using visual material and of operating in television studios. It arose more profoundly from the fear of the Editor of News that any attempt to make news visual would mean a lowering of news standards.

[ITN's first editor, Aidan] Crawley regarded personalisation in the presentation of news as an asset to be exploited, not as a crime to be avoided. So, though BBC news readers remained what they were called, men who read the news and had no hand in writing it, Independent Television News employed not news readers but 'newscasters' who from the first not only read the news but helped to edit and prepare it.

G. W. Goldie, *Facing the Nation: Television and Politics 1936–1976*, London: The Bodley Head, 1977, pp. 194, 197.

3.8   The roots of change: abandoning the 14-Day Rule

Amidst much discontent about the 14-Day Rule, a select committee was set up to review the issue. Although it recommended that the restrictions should be reduced to the minimum, not abandoned, it did comment that public debate encouraged an interest in Parliament and its work. Furthermore, it pointed out that the arrival of new channels of communication would make it more difficult to operate the rule. Initially, the rule was suspended for a period of six months from December 1956.

... Before withdrawing the rule, the Government obtained assurances from the BBC (and also from the ITA and the television programme companies) that they would continue to act in the spirit of the November resolution [that the principle of some limitation to the anticipation of parliamentary debates by broadcasting should be preserved], and in such a way as not to derogate from the primacy of Parliament as the forum for debating the affairs of the nation. The Corporation hopes that when the position is reviewed at the end of the trial period, the Government will find there is no justification for reimposing the Rule.

BBC, *Annual Report and Accounts 1956–57*, London: HMSO, Cmnd 267, October 1957, p. 19.

3.9   The roots of change: commercial television, the Suez crisis and election coverage

Broadcasters were beginning to assert themselves, driven perhaps by the zeal of the new commercial operators. Geoffrey

Cox, one-time editor at ITN, offers an insight into its ways of working.

Ever since 1945 the BBC had confined its coverage of the arguments put forward at elections to a summary of the manifesto of each party, and to the formal party political broadcasts, carefully allocated by agreement amongst those parties with a substantial number of candidates in the field. Apart from these, the only election news was on the movements of Party leaders and candidates and non-contentious information about the number of contestants and arrangements for polling....

Independent Television had not been on the air [during the April 1955 election] and none of the by-elections during 1955 and the early months of 1956 had been of sufficient interest for us to consider reporting their campaigns. Soon after Suez, however, a key by-election was called at Melton.... Not only did it provide the first gauge of public opinion since Suez, but it was in the seat vacated by Sir Anthony Nutting, who had resigned from the Foreign Office and from parliament as a protest against Eden's policy. It was clearly a story we should cover.

In planning its coverage ... the heart of the matter ... was the attitude of the main political parties.... We had to achieve, therefore, not so much a change in the Representation of the People Act as a change in the attitude of the politicians. The first step towards this was to demonstrate that television could cover elections fairly....

In these reports [from Melton, South Lewisham and Carmarthanshire] we evolved a pattern ... we showed scenes of the constituency to establish its nature; we interviewed voters ...; and in particular we interviewed the candidates ... so bringing the election argument for the first time clearly to the screen.

The next step was to apply these techniques to reporting an election whilst it was still in progress [i.e. Rochdale in 1958]....

We had learnt from our by-election coverage one further important lesson. The principle of fair shares must apply to the facilities used to cover a story as well as to minutes on the screen.... We were, in fact, applying in television terms the principle which the farsighted John Reith had laid down in 1923, that 'if on any controversial matter the opposing views are stated with equal emphasis and lucidity, there can at least be no charge of bias.' ...

A fortnight after the Rochdale by-election political broadcasting

took another step forward when for the first time a Prime Minister was interviewed at length on the air. Mr Harold Macmillan ... agreed to be interviewed on the BBC's 'Press Conference' and, three days later, by Robin Day.... No previous Prime Minister had been prepared to submit to interrogation outside the House of Commons.

G. Cox, *See it Happen: The Making of ITN*, London: The Bodley Head, 1983, pp. 113, 114–15, 117–18, 131.

3.10 Changes to the *Aide Mémoire*, and the rules of ministerial broadcasting

On 25 February 1969 the *Aide Mémoire* was revised again but this time the restrictions which were imposed in 1947 and 1948 were removed. The 1969 version restricted itself to ministerial broadcasts and removed the BBC's discretion in such matters.

1. In view of its executive responsibilities the Government of the day has the right to explain events to the public, or seek co-operation of the public, through the medium of broadcasting.

2. ... such occasions are of two kinds ...

3. The first category relates to Ministers wishing to explain legislation or administrative policies approved by Parliament, or to seek the co-operation of the public in matters where there is a general consensus of opinion. The BBC will provide suitable opportunities for such broadcasts within the regular framework of their programmes; there will be no right of reply by the Opposition.

4. The second category relates to more important and normally infrequent occasions, when the Prime Minister or one of his most senior Cabinet colleagues wishes to broadcast to the nation in order to provide information or explanation of events of prime national or international importance, or to seek the co-operation of the public in connection with such events.

5. The BBC will provide the Prime Minister or Cabinet Minister with suitable facilities on each occasion in this second category. Following such an occasion they may be asked to provide an equivalent opportunity for a broadcast by a leading Member of the Opposition, and will in that event do so.

6. When the opposition exercises this right to broadcast, there will follow as soon as possible, arranged by the BBC, a broadcast discussion of the issues between a member of the cabinet and a senior member of the opposition ...

Aide Mémoire, 25 February 1969, reproduced in J. Potter, *Independent Television in Britain: Volume III Politics and Expansion 1968–1980*, London: Macmillan, 1989, p. 319.

ELECTION COVERAGE

3.11   The Representation of the People Act

Two of broadcasting's election practices can be accounted for by reference to the Representation of the People Act. The first relates to the fact that broadcasting air-time cannot be bought on British television, so creating a more 'level playing field'; the second relates to election candidates' power of veto over broadcasts from their constituencies.

The 1949 Act made no mention of broadcasting. This was rectified by an Amendment to the Act in 1969 (Clause 9, 1969). The national, as opposed to local, nature of both modern election campaigns and media makes this clause rather old fashioned. This clause gives candidates power of veto over what can be broadcast, although broadcasters have learnt to overcome such obstacles by, for example, referring to all the candidates or not using any at all in constituency reports. Both these clauses are contained in the 1983 Act (Clauses 75 and 93 respectively).

Prohibition of expenses not authorised by election agent.
63.–(1) No expenses shall, with a view to promoting or procuring the election of a candidate at an election, be incurred by any person other than the candidate, his election agent and persons authorised ... on account –
 (a) of holding public meetings or organising any public display; or
 (b) of issuing advertisements, circulars or publications; or
 (c) of otherwise presenting to the electors the candidate or his views or the extent or nature of his backing or disparaging another candidate:

Provided that paragraph (c) of this section shall not –
(i) restrict the publication of any matter relating to the election in a newspaper or other periodical; ...

Representation of the People Act 1949, p. 1132.

Broadcasting during elections.
9.–(1) Pending a parliamentary or local government election, it shall not be lawful for any item about the constituency or electoral area to be broadcast ... if any of the ... candidates ... takes part in the item and the broadcast is not made with his consent; ...

Representation of the People Act 1969, p. 8.

3.12 The first party election broadcasts on television, 1951

David Butler's account of the use of television by politicians in 1951 is full of insights into what was taking place and the future impact of television on politics. Butler, it should be remembered, is describing 'live' and rehearsed broadcasts since the technology of television had not advanced sufficiently to allow for recordings or the more advanced video techniques of today.

The greatest innovation of the election was the use of television for party propaganda. Since this form of electioneering will undoubtedly be exploited far more in the future, it is worth devoting to it an amount of attention which may be out of proportion to the importance in 1951 of the three fifteen-minute performances which reached considerably less than 10% of the electorate....

When the BBC offered television facilities to the main parties in 1951 it was plainly conditional on both the main contestants agreeing to participate....

On this occasion ... the BBC offered each of the parties the use of the studio for a quarter of an hour's transmission and provided technical advice; the form of the programmes was left entirely to the parties.

Each of them made different use of the opportunity thus provided.

The Liberals, whose turn came first, were the most conventional; Lord Samuel appeared before the cameras by himself, and read a talk which may have been admirable, but which would have been just as well suited to radio as to television. Mr. Eden, who spoke for the Conservatives, brought with him Mr. Leslie Mitchell, a veteran television performer, to act as 'the common man' and to question him about Conservative policy. The Labour Party preferred to rely on a double team, Sir Hartley Shawcross and Mr. Christopher Mayhew, who took it in turns to speak directly to the cameras.

It is plain that the Liberals were the least successful.... It is no easy task for one person to hold the attention of a television audience uninterruptedly for fifteen minutes, and anyone who is seen to read what he has to say runs grave risks of destroying that sense of naturalness and intimacy which can make television so much the most potent medium of mass communication.

The Conservative effort was of a very different order. Viewers were able to watch Mr. Eden sitting easily at a desk while he was cross-questioned by Mr. Mitchell ... The main weakness of this part of the performance was that Mr. Mitchell's questions were a little too easy and 'stooge-ish' and at moments a certain spontaneity was lacking....

The Labour Party's tactics were very different, but they, too, made full use of ... [a] direct and personal approach to the viewer....

All the parties were, of course, relying on spokesmen who had had experience of being televised. It was perhaps natural that they should fight shy of the risk of finding their leaders untelegenic personalities. But public curiosity about the chief figures in each party is naturally very acute, and the opportunity of sending them canvassing personally in a million homes was so outstanding that one must wonder and regret that it was missed ...

D. Butler, *The British General Election of 1951*, London: Macmillan, 1952, pp. 75–8.

3.13 'Television elections': the arrangements for party election broadcasts

It is generally considered that the breakthrough in the coverage of elections came in 1958 when Granada Television, one of the ITV contractors, covered the by-election in Rochdale in February of that year. From then on, television broadcasters began to develop a variety of techniques to cover elections.

From these early, and uncertain, beginnings, party political broadcasts (PPBs) and party election broadcasts (PEBs) became a mainstay of political communication. In 1951 the allocation of time was equal across the three main political parties. In later years, the BBC and the main political parties would agree the allocation of time according to certain established criteria.

Significantly, it was the BBC (and then the other broadcasters) who offered the air-time – there are, in fact, no specific references to PEBs of PPBs in the BBC's Charter and Agreement. This had two interesting repercussions. First, it meant that in the mid-1980s when the then Social Democratic Party (SDP) came into prominence – but without any strength *in* Parliament – the BBC could take note of its standing in the country and offer it air-time (Negrine, 1994). Secondly, it also meant that what was offered could also be withdrawn, as the broadcasters planned to do in 1998 when they published proposals to do away with party election broadcasts (see 3.15).

18.17 The arrangements for party political broadcasting are at present based on agreement between the Broadcasting Authorities and the Labour, Conservative and Liberal parties, each of which is represented on the Committee on Party Political Broadcasting. The total amount of time for the broadcasts is agreed by the Committee each year on the basis of proposals put forward by the broadcasters, and the number of broadcasts given to a political party is governed in the first two years after a General Election by the amount of electoral support it received at the last election and, after that, two-thirds on the results of the General Election and one-third on the results of all subsequent by-elections. The broadcasts are arranged in two series ... and generally last either five or ten minutes....

18.18. When a General Election is announced, the regular series of party political broadcasts are suspended and the Committee on Party Political Broadcasting agree on the allocation of party election broadcasts. Parties not included in these arrangements may qualify for a broadcast if they have 50 or more candidates standing for election....

Report of the Committee on the Future of Broadcasting (Chairman: Lord Annan), London: HMSO, Cmnd 6753, March 1977, p. 297.

3.14   Reviewing the rules for PEBs and PPBs

The assessment given by the Annan Committee (above) offered a snapshot of practices up to that point in time. Subsequent events, including the general election of 1997, were to show just how difficult the task of allocating time to the political parties could be. In the 1997 general election the Referendum Party, the Pro-Life Alliance Party and Sinn Fein each took the BBC to court.

1974 Allocation rules revised – Allocation of broadcasting time for PPBs no longer to be determined by agreement between parties. Rules established – ten minutes for every two million votes at the previous election (with the SNP given ten minutes for every 200,000 votes and Plaid Cymru getting ten minutes for every 100,000)....

May 1996 *BBC sought Senior Counsel's advice on PEBs* – Two key points to emerge from the Conference were:

(i) Producers' Guidelines state that the BBC submit proposals to the Committee on Party Political Broadcasting. This is a fiction as the business of the Committee is conducted by Murdo Maclean, the Secretary to the Chief Whip. The obligation to be fair and consistent is the BBC's and if challenged in court the BBC must be clear about this.

(ii) A decision was taken to drop the concept of 'proven electoral support' for the minor parties and stick to a test of a minimum of 50 candidates....

Apr 1997 *Referendum Party took the BBC and ITC to Court* to seek judicial review of their decision to offer the Party only one five minute television and radio PEB. In his judgement, Lord Justice Auld dismissed the party's application saying that the broadcasters had acted in a 'reasonable' manner....

Jun 1997 *BBC and ITV wrote to the Secretary of the Committee on Party Political Broadcasting* thanking him for his services over the years and explaining that on legal advice it would be more appropriate for the BBC to receive representations directly from the various political parties rather than through the Committee....

Broadcasters Liaison Group, *Consultation Paper on the Reform of Party Political Broadcasting*, BBC/ITC/RA/S4C, 1998, Appendix 1.

3.15 Doing away with PPBs and PEBs: the broadcasters' proposals

Though never greatly popular, the broadcasts became even less popular in the 1990s. With heavier and heavier coverage of elections becoming the norm, a dislike of PEBs was not surprising. As they became slicker, more 'negative' and perhaps even emptier of content, their value could certainly be questioned. Were they still needed? The broadcasters' consultation paper of 1998 called for a review of the system.

Summary of Recommendations
Representations are, therefore, invited on proposals to:
  – Move the focus of party political broadcasting to election campaigns when the parties are directly seeking votes from the electorate.
  – Replace the annual series of PPBs with more PEBs to reflect the growth in the number of elected bodies in the UK.
  – Retain the system of PEBs for General Elections on the terrestrial TV networks, Radio 2 and Radio 4 with adjustments in Scotland and Wales and the three INR (Independent National Radio) services.
  – Introduce PEBs on BBC TV and Radio and UTV [Ulster Television] for the parties standing in Northern Ireland to replace the informal system of 'Campaign Broadcasts'.
  – Introduce a higher threshold of one sixth of seats contested, for the minor parties in all elections.
  – Establish a system of Election Broadcasts for the Scottish Parliament and Welsh Assembly.
  – Increase the number of Local Election Broadcasts for major parties on BBC1 and BBC2 and on ITV from one to two.
  – Review the system for European Elections ...
  – Cease Budget broadcasts, and concentrate opportunities for Ministerial broadcasts on truly exceptional circumstances.
  – Publish new ground rules covering editorial and compliance issues, and technical and delivery specifications.
  – Introduce a scheduling requirement by the ITC for broadcasters to place Party Election Broadcasts between 17.30 and 23.30 and

retain a commitment to prime time scheduling on the BBC.

Broadcasters Liaison Group, *Consultation Paper on the Reform of Party Political Broadcasting*, BBC/ITC/RA/S4C, 1998, p. 11.

3.16 The responsibilities of the broadcasting organisations # 1

The responsibilities of the broadcasting organisations derive from a number of key documents: the Royal Charter and the Licence and Agreement in the case of the BBC, the various Television Acts in the case of commercial television. The documents concerning the BBC are fairly general in kind and leave considerable room for the Corporation to interpret how its broadcasting obligations will be carried out. By contrast, the Television (latterly Broadcasting) Acts are more specific in kind.

A particularly significant clause which establishes the relationship between the government of the day and the BBC and commercial television companies is Clause 13(4) of the BBC's Licence and Agreement (and its equivalent in commercial television).

13(4) The Postmaster General may from time to time by notice in writing require the Corporation to refrain at any specified time or at all times from sending any matter or matters of any class specified in such notice; and the Postmaster General may at any time or times vary or revoke such a notice. The Corporation may at its discretion announce or refrain from announcing that such a notice has been given or has been varied or revoked.

BBC, *Handbook*, 1976, p. 290.

3.17 The responsibilities of the broadcasting organisations # 2

The Broadcasting White Paper of 1978 neatly summarised the obligations of the broadcasting organisations and their

sources of origin. Some of these derived from correspondence, e.g. the letter from Lord Normanbrook (dated 19 June
1964) containing assurances on political broadcasting.

101. The main obligations which are broadly common to the existing
broadcasting authorities in relation to the services and programmes
they provide are set out in the table below.

BBC	IBA
(1) Each Authority has a duty to provide its respective radio and television services as public services for the dissemination of information, education and entertainment, and to ensure that its programmes maintain a high general standard, in particular as respects their quality and content, and a proper balance and wide range of subject matter, having regard to the programmes as a whole and the days on which, and the times at which, programmes are broadcast.	
(BBC's Royal Charter, Article 3(a); Lord Normanbrook's letter)	(IBA Act 1973, section 2(2))
(2) Each Authority must ensure that, so far as possible, nothing is included in its programmes which offends against good taste or decency or is likely to encourage or incite to crime or lead to disorder or to be offensive to public feeling.	
(Lord Normanbrook's letter)	(section 4(1)(a))
(3a) The BBC must ensure that, so far as possible, due impartiality is preserved in news programmes dealing with matters of public policy, and also in the treatment of controversial subjects generally. (Lord Normanbrook's letter)	(3b) The IBA must ensure that, so far as possible ... all news is presented with due accuracy and impartiality. It must also ensure that, so far as possible, due impartiality is preserved on the part of persons providing the programmes as respects matters of political or industrial controversy or relating to public policy. (section 4(1)(b) and (f))
(4a) The BBC must ensure that programmes do not include any expression of the Corporation's	(4b) The IBA must ensure that programmes do not include any expression of the opinions of the

| opinions on current affairs or on matters of public policy. (Ministerial prescription under clause 13(4) of the Licence and Agreement) | Authority ... on matters of political or industrial controversy or relating to current policy. (section 4(2)) |

Home Office, *Broadcasting*, London: HMSO, Cmnd 7294, 1978, pp. 38–9.

TELEVISION IN THE HOUSE AND POLITICAL INTERVIEWS

3.18 One argument in favour of televising the Commons

Under the terms of the BBC's Licence and Agreement, the Corporation had to 'broadcast an impartial account day by day prepared by professional reporters of the proceedings in both Houses of ... Parliament' (Clause 13(2)). Such coverage, however, differed in kind from that to which Churchill, amongst other politicians, objected. Churchill's attitude reflected a fear that television would distort the workings of the House, that editing speeches would somehow destroy the seamless nature of debates, and that Parliament would be turned from a serious institution into a branch of light entertainment. Nevertheless, even in the late 1950s, there were some who were prepared to think the unthinkable, namely that television should be allowed into the House of Commons.

It was Aneurin Bevan who introduced the matter in 1959 with a set of points which were as pertinent in the 1980s.

It was said last week that there was a considerable gulf growing between this House and the nation. I believe that to be absolutely true. There is lessening interest in our discussions. We are not reaching the country to the extent that we did. It can no longer be argued that the national newspapers are means of communication between the House of Commons and the public. The fact is that Parliamentary reporting has become a sheer travesty. Apart from a few responsible, solid newspapers with small circulations, the debates in this House are hardly reported at all, and such reports as take place are ... a complete travesty of our proceedings....

The same can be said of the radio and even more can be said of television.... In fact, there has been nothing more humiliating than to see Members of Parliament in responsible positions selected by unrepresentative persons to have an opportunity of appearing on the radio and television....

Also, what is almost worse, political alternatives are not placed before the people in a realistic fashion because of the selection of speakers that takes place.... At the beginning of this Parliament I am going to suggest that a serious investigation takes place into the technical possibilities of televising Parliamentary proceedings.

Mr Cyril Osborne (Louth): Oh, no, Nye.

Mr Bevan: I know that Hon. Members shake their heads, but why should they be so shy? Would it not be an excellent thing if ... speeches ... were heard by ... constituents?... All I am suggesting is that in these days when all the apparatus of mass suggestion are against democratic education, we should seriously consider re-establishing intelligent communication between the House of Commons and the Electorate as a whole. That, surely, is a democratic process.

House of Commons Debates, 3 November 1959, vol. 612, cols 865–7.

3.19 A 'Television Hansard'

Concerns about how television would treat Parliament, and what it would do to both Parliament and MPs, ensured that the motion would be defeated. As even Robin Day admitted, Bevan's idea of a continuous channel of parliamentary debate was not one that would gain much favour. Day's favourite option was an edited programme of extracts from the House – but a key consideration for MPs was who was to do the editing. On the whole, MPs were not inclined to trust broadcasters. For Colin Seymour-Ure, the key issue was whether broadcasting was 'bigger' than Parliament (1974: 149–50).

It seemed to me that an alternative method [to a continuous channel] was much more likely to gain acceptance – a late evening 'Television Hansard', which would be an *edited* recording of the day's proceedings, varying in length according to what happened....

The case for a 'Television Hansard' is inspired by respect for the institution of Parliament. For how can Parliament maintain its rightful importance as the nation's prime forum of debate, if it shuts itself off from the nation's prime medium of communication?

R. Day, *The Case for Televising Parliament*, London: Hansard Society, 1963, pp. 7, 21. Reprinted in R. Day, *Day by Day*, London: William Kimber, 1975, pp. 120, 136.

3.20   The birth of the television interview: Robin Day and Harold Macmillan

Despite Day's comments concerning Parliament as 'the prime forum of debate', his own work as a television interviewer transformed the television studio into the prime forum. Although Day considers his interview with Harold Macmillan on 23 February 1958 a historic one, as historic was his interview with President Nasser of Egypt a year earlier. Both interviews are significant milestones in the development of British broadcast journalism.

My interview with Macmillan lasted thirteen minutes.... The interview ... was historic and unprecedented. No one had previously interrogated a Prime Minister in this way outside Parliament....

This ... was the first time a Prime Minister had been vigorously questioned on television. The interview was also the first in which a Prime Minister had been questioned by a single interviewer, apart from brief interviews at airports....

The significance of my ITN interview with Macmillan is difficult to convey today. Here was the nation's leader, the most powerful and important politician of the time, coming to terms with the new medium of television. He was questioned on TV as vigorously as in Parliament. His TV performance that Sunday evening was an early recognition that television was not merely for entertainment or party propagandists, but was now a serious part of the democratic process.

R. Day, *Grand Inquisitor*, London: Pan Books, 1989, pp. 2–3.

3.21   The birth of the television interview: Robin Day and President Nasser

The interview with President Nasser of Egypt took place in July 1957, several months after the British-French-Israeli assault on Egypt following Egypt's nationalisation of the Suez Canal. The interview lasted twenty minutes but its repercussions were noted by the journalist James Cameron.

Sitting in the garden of his Cairo home, President Nasser leaned forward last night into British television screens. And he asked that we reunite in friendly relations. He thus did something that had never been done before in the history of international diplomacy.

For the first time on record, a national leader submitting a major point of national policy, by-passed all protocol and sent his message into the homes of another state *at a time when the two were not in diplomatic relations.*

News Chronicle, 2 July 1957. Quoted in R. Day, *Grand Inquisitor*, London: Pan Books, 1989, p. 109.

3.22   Concerns about televising the Commons

Debates about televising the Commons continued well into the 1980s and alongside the growing importance of the television studio as a forum for political debate. There were debates in 1972, 1974, 1975, 1978, 1980, 1981 and 1983, but in none of these was the motion to televise the Commons carried. In 1985 Miss Janet Fookes moved the motion in favour of televising the House of Commons. The arguments put in favour of the motion were no different from those put forward in 1960s.

(Janet Fookes) ... If we allow the cameras in, we shall move forward well into the 20th century ... we must face the fact that many members of the public rely mainly on television for their information about politics. It was estimated in a recent poll that 62 per cent of the people say that most of their information comes from television – (HON. MEMBERS: 'Disgraceful.') Disgraceful or not, we have to deal with the facts. If it is a fact that most people gain their information from television, we are losing badly by not having television cameras in the Chamber.

(Edward Heath) I maintain this position [to allow cameras access] as a principle of democracy. The proceedings of the governing body should be widely communicated as speedily as possible. I maintain it also as a principal right of the citizen to know as quickly as possible the details of the proceedings of the governing body.... Our responsibility must be to make our proceedings as widely available as possible.

House of Commons Debates, 20 November 1985, vol. 87, no. 11, cols 279, 287.

3.23   The decline in the reporting of Parliament

Those who supported the 1985 motion failed to persuade a majority of MPs and the motion was defeated by 263 votes to 275. But one interesting addition to the debate was a contribution by Alan Beith which, in retrospect, underlines the House's dilemma.

... There has clearly been a decline in what we call the Gallery reporting of Parliament – the extent to which newspapers report our debates and seek to set out what is said.... Only two or perhaps three serious newspapers have regular Gallery columns, reporting systematically the proceedings of the House. The reports seem to get shorter and shorter and occupy less and less space. The rest of the reporting of Parliament, apart from the news contributions of political correspondents and the parliamentary sketches, which themselves have changed, depends on the occasional line here and there....

This considerable change in press reporting has been reflected in broadcasting....

These are the facts of life. They will happen tomorrow without the House being televised, but because of them we have to ask questions about how the televising of the House might be carried out.

House of Commons Debates, 20 November 1985, vol. 87, no. 11, col. 291.

3.24   Television in the House, almost

By the time of the next debate, in February 1988, the Lords was being televised and sound broadcasting from the Commons was a common feature of news programmes. The motion for 'an experiment into televising the proceedings of the House and the establishment of a Select Committee to decide how best to implement that' was passed with 318 votes for and 264 against (*House of Commons Debates*, 9 February 1988, vol. 127). There was still concern about coverage though, as can be seen in John Wakeham's speech in favour of the report of the Select Committee on the Televising of the Commons.

The essence of our proposals is that the House should retain overall control, including control of the rules of coverage.

Our proposals [regarding the rules of coverage] have been given a hostile reception. Those who have expressed their views most vociferously are the representatives of the media, who can hardly be said to be disinterested observers.

The director (or programmes) should seek, in close collaboration with the Supervisor of Broadcasting, to give a full, balanced, fair and accurate account of proceedings, with the aim of informing viewers about the work of the House.

The words 'full, balanced, fair and accurate account' were carefully chosen to describe the type of coverage which the Select Committee believed to be desirable. It is, of course, precisely in the interpretation of this phrase that the differences of perspective have emerged between the broadcasters and the committee. The broadcasters – for perfectly legitimate and understandable reasons – see it as their right and duty to film what happens in the Chamber in exactly the same way as they would an election meeting or party conference, with full journalistic licence to cut away from the speaker who has the floor to paint an impressionistic picture by the use of a range of different camera shots and editorial techniques.

By contrast, the Select Committee felt ... that the purpose of television coverage should be to provide something like an 'electronic Hansard', designed to provide viewers with a factual and objective visual record of our proceedings – of speeches and statements made, of questions asked and answered and of decisions taken.

House of Commons Debates, 12 June 1989, vol. 154, cols 608–9.

3.25 Cameras in the House, but where is the press?

Ironically, no sooner had cameras been introduced into the
House than the broadsheet press – or the rump of it that continued to use Gallery reporters to record debates and the like
– decided that it no longer needed that service for its readers
and that Parliament should be treated mainly as a source of
political *news*. Not surprisingly, some MPs were seriously
concerned that the media were no longer showing the public
the full working character of Parliament. This was the view of
Jack Straw, the Labour MP (and it justified Alan Beith's comments in 3.23).

[T]he quantity of reporting declined a little between 1933 and 1988,
and its style altered. But the fundamental nature and content of the
reporting remained the same. The purpose was to report what happened in the Chamber of the Commons....

In the last five years, however, the reporting of Parliament has
undergone a greater change than at any time in the last 60 years, and
probably the last century. The systematic reporting of debate has all
but been abandoned. Newspapers like *The Times* and *The Guardian*,
which claim most to want to uphold, and strengthen, the Parliamentary process, have been among the worst offenders. Their coverage
has been cut to a quarter of what it was even in the very recent past....

The decline in press reporting ... would appear to have a number
of linked causes. These include:

• the televising of parliament (from 1989). This ... led some newspaper executives to assert that there is no need to report what was
anyway available on television. But there is a double paradox here.
First, the newspapers continue to give prominence to exactly the
same small parts of Parliamentary proceedings ... which also form the
basis of radio and TV reports of parliament. Secondly, this very concentration by radio and TV on Prime Minister's Questions seems to
have reinforced the view among some editors and executives that Parliament was simply a slanging and shouting match which therefore
deserved even less coverage than it had previously received....

• a delayed reaction to the very large majorities of the 'Thatcher

Years'. This meant that whatever the quality of the debate and the weight of the argument, the government was always assured of a majority....

• a generation change among political editors of the broadsheet papers. Coincidentally, many senior political editors, brought up on Gallery reporting, retired or moved on in the mid '80s. The new approach of their replacements reinforced the view, led by the then new *Independent*, that straight Gallery reporting was boring, and should in part be replaced by 'colour' and 'Lobby' pieces;

• a consequential change in the behaviour of MPs. They have resorted more and more to the press release in the near absence of any coverage of Chamber speeches which they make.

Jack Straw, MP, *The Decline in Press Reporting of Parliament*, October 1993, pp. 4, 5.

3.26 One reason for the decline in coverage: the editor's view

Simon Jenkins, former editor of *The Times*, appeared in front of the Nolan Committee in 1995 and explained his reasons for dropping the parliamentary page.

TOM KING: ... If you look at your own newspaper [*The Times*], ... that used to have a full page of Parliamentary report. It now has nothing.... Do you think that is right?

SIMON JENKINS: Yes, I took the decision to stop it. I stopped it because I couldn't find who read it apart from MPs. We are not there to provide a public service for a particular profession or, for that matter, for a particular legislative chamber. The House of Lords had always felt hard-done-by in the same respect. Newspapers are about providing people with news....

TOM KING: Sorry, newspapers are about writing good news, is that it?

SIMON JENKINS: Providing news. Up to a point news that people want to read. But if you are asking a slightly different question, which is 'Is the coverage of politics in newspapers an accurate reflection of the shifts of power within government?' I think I'd agree with you that it probably isn't – it isn't – because it focuses too much on what happens in Westminster and too little on what happens in Whitehall. And one of the consequences of that is that an excessively searching spotlight is fastened on MPs. You can't have it both ways. I believe myself that the centre of gravity of political journalism still tends to be too much focused on the corridors of Westminster and not enough over the road in Whitehall.

TOM KING: ... I am actually struck by the amount of people who actually watch the morning programme on BBC2 and others, reporting on Parliament ... An audience which you feel actually doesn't exist?

SIMON JENKINS: Well, people who want to read, not watch or hear, but read, what goes on in Parliament can subscribe to Hansard. The extent to which they appeared to want to read large amounts of material of MPs making speeches in the House, I believed was limited. And that was my judgement and it is the judgement, I think, of other editors, too.

Committee on Standards in Public Life (Nolan Committee), *First Report, Transcripts of Oral Evidence*, London: HMSO, Cm 2850-II, 17 January 1995, p. 7.

MOMENTS OF CRISIS IN THE RELATIONSHIP BETWEEN BROADCASTERS AND POLITICIANS

The Suez crisis in 1956 brought the BBC into conflict with the government of Anthony Eden and produced yet one more example of the difficult relationship that existed (and still exists) between the broadcasters and those in authority. The events surrounding the take-over of the Suez Canal by President Nasser of Egypt highlighted a number of different aspects of the relationship between the broadcasters and the government. First, and as research has subsequently shown, it paints a picture of a BBC operating under considerable pressure from the Prime Minister and his colleagues (see Briggs, 1995; Shaw, 1996). Second, it shows that the BBC was, in general, not as impartial in its handling of the crisis as is often portrayed (Shaw, 1996); third, that the BBC was implicated in some aspects of government propaganda in the Middle East (Norton-Taylor, 1994); and, fourth, that despite all the above, it was able to use the existing rules of coverage as contained in the *Aide Mémoire* of 1947 to create a space for dissent and debate over the government's handling of the crisis, its collusion with France and its military adventure. One additional aspect is also important, namely, that by reporting and commenting on events contrary to the 14-Day Rule, the BBC and ITN brought to a close its short, and ignominious, life.

3.27 Pressure from government, 1956

Anthony Eden deeply distrusted the BBC; at a particularly difficult moment during the early part of the Suez crisis he asked his Press Secretary: 'Are they enemies or just socialists?' (quoted in Shaw, 1996: 112). His efforts to 'guide' the BBC's handling of the coverage was not without success, but it was a success brought about by sustained pressure and threats. A letter to Sir Alexander Cadogan, Chairman of the BBC Board of Governors, reflects the atmosphere and is very similar to other communications between governments and the BBC (see 3.33).

My Dear Alec, since we spoke on the telephone last night about Major Salem's broadcast I have had several reports of the programme in which he spoke. All of these reports have been critical, and I have heard that the programme gave a deplorably misleading picture of British opinion as uncertain and hesitant....

Of course the Government have no intention of interfering with the freedom of the BBC to try to reflect, as well as educate, public opinion in this country. But I hope the Governors will bear in mind the very heavy responsibility which rests on the BBC at this crucial time when an international conference is meeting in London. Many people will judge the strength and determination of Britain by what they hear on the BBC....

I do not need to tell you how grave the present crisis is for this country and the whole of the western world. This is not a Prime Minister's representation but a personal comment which I thought you should have in view of our talk about this programme last night.

Eden to Cadogan, 16 August 1956, quoted in T. Shaw, *Eden, Suez and the Mass Media*, London: I. B. Taurus, 1996, pp. 119–20.

3.28 Controversial broadcasts and the *Aide Mémoire*

The *Aide Mémoire* stipulated that if a broadcast was made by a minister which was deemed to be controversial, the Opposition could request to make a reply to the broadcast (see above, pp. 102–3). A balance of sorts could thus be struck between the government and the Opposition in matters of public controversy. Suez was one such instance: it could not avoid broadcasting the very real divisions of opinion about the handling of the crisis not only in Parliament but also in the public arena. An added difficulty for the BBC was that it had to balance its role as a domestic broadcaster with its role as an international (radio) broadcaster.

At no time since broadcasting began had there been such a lack of agreement in Parliament and the country on a major matter of foreign policy. Never previously, therefore, had the BBC's tradition of objective reporting, in its external as in its home programmes, [been required] to show to the world a large part of the nation deeply critical of the Government of the day on a matter of vital national concern.

There were many, in Parliament and elsewhere, who thought that the BBC was wrong to maintain its traditional policy in these circumstances. They felt that the national interest would be best served by ignoring, in external broadcasts at least, the wide division of opinion in the country. The Corporation could not accept that view. In the first place, it believed that for the BBC to have been found for the first time suppressing important items of news – and it could not have done so unnoticed abroad – would have been to destroy its own reputation without vindicating that of the Government, and that the harm done to the national interest in that event would far have outweighed any damage caused by displaying to the world the workings of a free democracy. Secondly, the Corporation felt sure that the BBC's critics were obscuring the difference between news and comment, for while news could not be otherwise than objective and impartial, in comment it was possible to put the British case for action forcefully and effectively. Evidence reaching the Corporation since the Suez crisis has shown not only that the BBC's continued adherence to honest reporting during the crucial period was greatly respected abroad, but also that the vigorous presentation by BBC commentators of the reasons for Britain's action in Egypt did much to promote a better understanding of it even among those who were bitterly opposed.

BBC, *Annual Report and Accounts 1956–57*, London: HMSO, Cmnd 267, October 1957, pp. 15–16.

3.29 The lessons of Suez

The public divisions were aired not only in the broadcast media but also in the press. Some newspapers, such as the *Daily Mirror*, were not only strongly against military intervention in Egypt but also called for the Prime Minister's resignation (see Negrine, 1982). But as the crisis deepened and as the BBC (television service) continued to provide venues for debate and discussion, it felt the pressure from many different quarters: from prime ministerial level (with threats), and from Opposition (for a share of broadcast time). Consequently, when Eden requested another ministerial broadcast (on 3 November 1956), the Labour Party also requested airtime.

[The Labour Party] immediately demanded a right of reply. The BBC now came under severe pressure from both political parties. There was no agreement between them that the Prime Minister's broadcast had been 'controversial' in the sense of the *Aide Mémoire*. So the BBC had to 'exercise its own judgement' about a right of reply....

Suez is, therefore, a salutary warning of the lengths to which a political party may go, when in power, to prevent the broadcasting of any opinions but its own. It also reveals the importance of maintaining procedures, agreed in advance by broadcasters and Opposition as well as by Government, to which the broadcasting organisations can refer when refusing to submit to government pressures exerted at moments of tension when emotions are running high.

G. W. Goldie, *Facing the Nation: Television and Politics 1936–1976*, London: The Bodley Head, 1977, pp. 182, 186.

The political issue of Ulster has consistently troubled broadcasters and has provided many examples of 'problem' programmes such as *The Question of Ulster* (1972), the Carrickmore 'incident' (1979) and *Death on the Rock* (1988). All these had major consequences for the broadcasters. *Real Lives: At the Edge of the Union* (1986) stands out in that it brought about the first one-day strike by journalists in the history of the BBC.

Was there an obvious pattern behind all these, and other, programmes? The simplest answer is that they all questioned the manner in which the issue of Ireland was being dealt with and, in their own way, they attempted to give a public platform to voices which were otherwise rarely heard. Clearly, however, in the context of the Prevention of Terrorism Act and the Broadcasting Ban (1988) these aims might be seen by many as naive, to say the least.

3.30   The BBC's *The Question of Ulster*

One early sign of the very problematic nature of programmes on Ireland came in 1972 – only five or so years after the 'troubles' began – when the BBC proposed to broadcast a programme which sought to review and analyse the issue. The programme, devised as an inquiry or tribunal, was called *The Question of Ulster*. In his memoirs, Lord Hill, then Chair of the BBC Board of Governors, sets out the broader context of such programming.

Yet another controversy about the BBC's handling of Northern Ireland arose in November (1971).... The Board of Governors had discussed some aspect of programmes about this unhappy province at almost every meeting. It was perhaps inevitable ... that those who sought to report what they found, however faithfully, should be under fire. There had been frequent allegations of bias, or misrepresentation, even of encouraging the terrorists by interviewing members of the IRA....

To reduce the danger of error, the director-general had instructed that no IRA member should be interviewed without his express permission, subsequently delegating to the editor of news and current affairs the power of approval. He had introduced a system of greater supervision.

Although the amount of criticism had declined, the situation was still delicate and the mood uncertain.... Some backbenchers pressed the Home Secretary, Reginald Maudling, to impose some form of 'patriotic censorship' on BBC television and newspaper reporting of the Northern Ireland troubles....

[In a meeting with the Home Secretary] I suggested, as a sensible procedure, that I should reply to the points of criticism made at the meeting of backbenchers in a letter which would be published.

[The letter included a defence of the BBC's position and a strong argument against censorship. But it also contained a paragraph which was to cause rumbles within the organisation.]

In short, as between the government and the opposition, as between the two communities in Northern Ireland, the BBC has a duty to be impartial no less than in the rest of the United Kingdom. But, as between the British Army and the gunmen the BBC is not and cannot be impartial....

What they [the journalists within the BBC who objected to Hill's paragraph regarding the gunmen] don't seem to see is that we are fighting a battle against censorship, control, regulation, intervention from outside. The claim of programme makers in news, current affairs or in any other field that they should decide what goes on the screen or emerges from the microphone without guidance or instruction from above, is just the sort of claim that brings external control nearer.

C. Hill, *Behind the Screen: The Broadcasting Memoirs of Lord Hill*, London: Sidgwick & Jackson, 1974, pp. 207–11.

3.31 Reporting Northern Ireland: *The Question of Ulster*

Lord Hill's view of the relationship of the BBC to the state and other political actors did not prevent him from championing the programme *The Question of Ulster*. He, and the Director General of the BBC, were kept fully informed of its development and he was also involved in discussions about its structure. Nevertheless, the Home Secretary, Reginald Maudling, and the Fleet Street press began to raise doubts about its transmission. Maudling asked to see Hill on 13 December 1971.

The Home Secretary ... said he was seriously disquieted by the project, which he regarded as potentially dangerous, quite apart from his view that it had a built-in bias....

I replied that the programme was a genuine attempt to present a fair picture from a variety of angles. I thought the programme would be valuable, and could not agree to abandon it, though the governors would consider Mr Maudling's views about balance....

On Monday 3 January [1972] I presided over another meeting with five governors and others at Broadcasting House, and, subject to consultation on the telephone with absent governors, the go-ahead [to transmit the programme] was given....

Next day the Home Secretary took an unprecedented step. He sent me a letter, by hand, saying that he would later send it to the press, declaring that he believed the programme 'in the form in which it had been devised could do no good and could do serious harm'....

As a result of the newspaper campaign and the Home Secretary's letter, the programme got a much bigger audience than would normally be expected....

C. Hill, *Behind the Screen: The Broadcasting Memoirs of Lord Hill*, London: Sidgwick & Jackson, 1974, pp. 219–21.

3.32 Reporting Northern Ireland: *Real Lives: At the Edge of the Union* # 1

'Real Lives' was a series of programmes which simply documented people's lives. It was not intended to be an inquisitorial, in-depth assessment of what they did or where they stood. The particular programme which caused upheaval, *At the Edge of the Union*, focused on two men from Northern Ireland who stood on each side of the divide: Martin McGuiness and Gregory Campbell. William Rees-Mogg, then Vice-Chairman of the BBC Board of Governors, explained his own dislike of the programme.

The 'fly-on-the-wall' technique which the whole of the series of Real Lives was using meant that no questions were put to anybody. They were just allowed to talk. They were filmed; they were filmed with their families in very sympathetic circumstances and they put their own case in their own words with no questions being put to them to test that case.

So I thought that it just made the terrorist look just a nice guy. You saw him with his family and a man with his family, and any man with his children on his knee looks a pleasant human being and he certainly did.

I thought it concealed the real nature of the man, which is to kill people.

Rees-Mogg interviewed in 1988. Quoted in *History of the BBC: 75 Years of the BBC*, BBC television programme, 1998.

3.33   Reporting Northern Ireland: *Real Lives: At the Edge of the Union # 2*

Leon Brittan, Home Secretary, held similar views. These were conveyed to the Chair of the BBC Board of Governors. The letter illustrates quite dramatically the very subtle relationship which exists between the BBC and the government of the day.

Dear Stuart [Young],
I was very glad to learn that you and your colleagues are considering whether or not to proceed with the broadcast of the proposed 'Real Lives' programme involving Martin McGuinness and Gregory Campbell. This letter confirms the views which I asked Wilfrid Hyde to convey on my behalf to the Corporation this morning.

May I first make it quite clear that I unhesitatingly accept that the decision to broadcast or to refrain from broadcasting this programme must rest exclusively with the Corporation.

It is no part of my task as the minister responsible for broadcasting policy generally to attempt to impose an act of censorship on what should be broadcast in particular programmes. To do so would rightly be inconsistent with the constitutional independence of the BBC, which is a crucial part of our broadcasting arrangements.

I do, on the other hand, also have a ministerial responsibility for the fight against the ever present threat of terrorism, and I would be failing in my duty if I did not let you and your colleagues have my considered views on the impact of this programme in that context.

[The programme] ... will enable McGuinness to advocate or justify the use of violence for political ends, and thus the murder and maiming of innocent people, before a huge public audience. He will, moreover, be doing so not in the course of a theoretical debate about terrorism, but as a prominent apologist of an organisation that is proud to have carried out murders and such maimings and expresses its readiness and intention to carry out more. The BBC would be giving an immensely valuable platform to those who have evinced an ability to murder indiscriminately its own viewers.

Quite apart from the deep offence that this would give the overwhelming majority of the population and the profound distress that it would cause to families of the victims of terrorism, it would also in my considered judgement materially assist the terrorist cause....

... Even if the programme and any surrounding material were, as a whole, to present terrorist organisations in a wholly unfavourable light, I would still ask you not to permit it to be broadcast. For the gain that the terrorist would secure by the broadcast would not be the conversion of large numbers of people to their cause, but the opportunity to boost the morale of their supporters and to alarm the innocent majority who have every reason to fear their intentions.

It must be damaging to security and therefore wholly contrary to the public interest to provide a boost to the morale of the terrorists and their apologists in this way. I cannot believe the BBC would wish to give succour to terrorist organisations: and it is for this reason that I hope that you and your colleagues will agree on reflection that the 'Real Lives' programme should not be broadcast.

Letter from Leon Brittan, Home Secretary, to Stuart Young, Chairman of the BBC, 29 July 1985. Quoted in R. Bolton, *Death on the Rock*, London: W. H. Allen, 1990, pp. 160–2.

3.34   Reporting Northern Ireland: the Broadcasting Ban, 1988

Programmes about Ireland continued to trouble the broadcasters throughout the 1980s. Many programmes were changed or dropped as a way of avoiding trouble (see Curtis, 1984), but it was not until 1988 that a government felt strongly enough about the coverage of Ireland, and of terrorists in particular, to impose an actual ban. On 19 October 1988 the Home Secretary, Douglas Hurd, announced a ban on the use of the direct speech of terrorists on any broadcasting services. To get around the ban, broadcasters simply dubbed the words of those prevented from having their words reach the audience directly. Significantly, there were no parallel restrictions imposed on newspapers. This ban was withdrawn in 1994, when the 'troubles' in Ireland abated.

For some time, broadcast coverage of events in Northern Ireland has included the occasional appearance of representatives of paramilitary organisations and their political wings, who have used these opportunities as an attempt to justify their criminal activities. Such appearances have caused widespread offence to viewers and listeners throughout the United Kingdom, particularly just after a terrorist outrage.

The terrorists themselves draw support and sustenance from access to radio and television – from addressing their views more directly to the population at large than is possible through the press. The Government have decided that the time has come to deny this easy platform to those who use it to propagate terrorism. Accordingly, I have today issued to the chairmen of the BBC and the IBA a notice, under the licence and agreement and under the Broadcasting Act 1987 respectively, requiring them to refrain from broadcasting direct statements by representatives of organisations proscribed in Northern Ireland and Great Britain and by representatives of Sinn Fein, Republican Sinn Fein and the Ulster Defence Association. The notices will also prohibit the broadcasting of statements by any person which support or invite support for these organisations....

... The wording of the notice ... is that we are talking about words spoken by a person who appears or is heard on the programme on which the matter is broadcast where the person speaking the words represents, or purports to represent, one of the organisations specified.

Douglas Hurd, *House of Commons Debates*, 19 October 1988, vol. 138, cols 893, 901.

4

The British press, 1945–1998

The extracts included in this chapter focus almost entirely on the national newspaper industry. They have been chosen to reflect the many concerns which have lain behind some of the commentaries on the industry and its 'problems': problems variously identified in the more recent past as relating to a lack of sufficient advertising revenue to go round, an intensely competitive industry, inadequate management, overmanning and an excess of labour union power, and the absence of the most up-to-date technology in the production process.

There is much that does not appear in this chapter: changes in ownership, changes in editorial personnel, changes in pricing. There have been too many of these sorts of changes to document but – and this is also significant – since there has been no inquiry into the industry in well over twenty years, there has been no official or comprehensive documentation of the totality of change produced outside academic commentary. Extracts from the latter category of texts have been kept to a minimum.

In spite of the many reviews of the industry that have been conducted, the newspaper industry remains competitive and the concern about its future – or perhaps more correctly the future of some titles – remains undimmed. One other thing remains unchanged across the period under review and that is the strong attachment in various 'official' documents to the belief that any state intervention whatsoever is likely to damage the 'freedom of the press'.

4.1 Royal Commissions on the Press

Since 1945, there have been three Royal Commissions on the Press (1947–49, 1961–62, 1974–77). The first Royal

Commission was established during a period of newsprint shortages and rationing.

14. Some account of the circumstances in which we were appointed is necessary to an understanding of the character of our inquiry. The demand for a Royal Commission was initiated by the National Union of Journalists. It came before the House of Commons on 29th October, 1946, when two Members, both journalists, moved the following motion:

That, having regard to the increasing public concern at the growth of monopolistic tendencies in the control of the Press and with the object of furthering the free expression of opinion through the Press and the greatest practicable accuracy in the presentation of news this House considers that a Royal Commission should be appointed to inquire into the finance, control, management and ownership of the Press....

18. Our Terms of Reference required us 'with the object of furthering the free expression of opinion through the Press and the greatest practicable accuracy in the presentation of news, to inquire into the control, management and ownership of the newspaper and periodical Press and the news agencies, including the financial structure and the monopolistic tendencies in control, and to make recommendations thereon.' Our functions were thus doubly defined. The subject matter was the control, management, and ownership of the newspaper and periodical Press and the news agencies: the purpose was the furtherance of the free expression of opinion and the greatest practicable accuracy in the presentation of news. Guided by these bearings, we concentrated our investigations on the questions which appeared to be central to the problem before us:

(i) what degree of concentration of ownership of newspapers, periodicals, and news agencies at present exists;

(ii) whether there is a tendency towards further concentration;

(iii) whether such concentration as exists is on balance disadvantageous to the free expression of opinion or the accurate presentation of news;

(iv) whether any other factors in the control, management, or ownership of the Press or of the news agencies, or any external influences operating on those concerned in control, management, or ownership, militate against this freedom and accuracy; and

(v) how this freedom and accuracy may best be promoted.

Royal Commission on the Press 1947–49 (Chairman: Sir W. D. Ross), *Report*, London: HMSO, Cmd 7700, June 1949, pp. 1, 3–5.

4.2 The standard by which the press should be judged (1947–49)

The 1947–49 Royal Commission set out three 'standards by which the press should be judged'. The first was judging the press as 'the chief agency for instructing the public on the main issues of the day' (p. 100, para. 361), the second standard related to its ability and competence in reporting news, and the third 'regards the press less as a public service than as a great industry concerned with the collection and diffusion of news' (p. 103, para. 371). Though more general, the first standard provides an overview of the duties of the press (and the media).

The Press as an instrument of information and instruction
362. The democratic form of society demands of its members an active and intelligent participation in the affairs of their community, whether local or national. It assumes that they are sufficiently well informed about the issues of the day to be able to form the broad judgements required by an election, ... it demands also an alert and informed participation not only in purely political processes but also in the efforts of the community to adjust its social and economic life to increasingly complex circumstances. Democratic society, therefore, needs a clear and truthful account of events, of their background and their causes; a forum for discussion and informed criticism; and a means whereby individuals and groups can express a point of view or advocate a cause....

The Press's standard for itself ...
[With respect to the second standard]
368. While there was general agreement that a newspaper has a right, and possibly a duty, to formulate and express its own opinions, there was some difference [amongst publishers] on the question whether, and to what extent, it should publish those of others. It was generally agreed on the one hand that, in the words of Odhams Press Ltd., 'there is no obligation on any of the several units of the Press to

provide a universal platform' for the propagation of ideas, and on the other that opinions which by reason either of their importance or of their general interest have become news, ought to be reported whether or not the newspapers agree with them. Some undertakings thought that this was as far as a paper was bound to go and that it was under no obligation in ventilating a particular topic to present opinions upon it other than its own....

370. There was general, and frequently emphatic, agreement that news and opinion should be strictly separated, qualified in some cases only by the suggestion that, especially in newspapers of the present size, some news may be contained in opinion columns, and by reservations for the articles of specialists such as political or industrial correspondents....

The Press as an industry
371. The third standard by which the Press may be judged regards the Press less as a public service than as a great industry concerned with the collection and diffusion of news. ...

The standard to be applied
377. In our view no standard of judgement can be wholly relevant which fails to take some account of the bases both of the first of these standards and of the third. The Press is not purely an agency for the political education of the public, much though democratic society may need such an agency. On the other hand, it cannot be considered purely as an industry: the inescapable fact that it is the main source of information, discussion, and advocacy imposes upon it responsibilities greater than those resting on an industry which does not deal in information and ideas.

378. The first standard fails to allow for the fact that the primary business of a newspaper undertaking is to sell newspapers. Only by selling newspapers can such an undertaking maintain its existence....

380. The first standard is not, therefore, wholly relevant: but if it is set too high, the third may be set too low. Though a newspaper is a commercial enterprise it does not follow that it need necessarily pursue commercial advantage without limit. A newspaper whose financial position is precarious will, it is true, be compelled to concern itself almost entirely with money-making; but a successful undertaking seldom aims exclusively at profit; it is also interested in its own conception of success, and that conception may include a regard for

the responsibilities imposed on the Press by the part it plays in the life of the community....

383. There are ... two essential requirements which in our view newspapers individually and the Press collectively ought to fulfil....

384. The first of these requirements is that if a newspaper purports to record and discuss public affairs, it should at least record them truthfully.... The second requirement is that the number and variety of newspapers should be such that the Press as a whole gives an opportunity for all important points of view to be effectively presented in terms of the varying standards of taste, political opinion, and education among the principal groups of the population.

385. These two requirements are not stated as alternatives: they are complementary. We recognise that even if they are satisfied, the pre-occupations of the Press with the exceptional, and the limited range of interests of the readers of any paper, must continue to throw the picture of events presented by the Press out of focus; but if the Press gives its readers the means of forming judgements on the problems of most immediate interest to them, that is perhaps as much as need be asked of it at present.

Royal Commission on the Press 1947–49 (Chairman: Sir W. D. Ross), *Report*, London: HMSO, Cmd 7700, June 1949, pp. 100–6.

4.3 Judging the health of the newspaper industry in the 1940s

> The 'central questions' which the 1947–49 Commission set out to investigate forced it to deal with such issues as concentration of ownership, newspaper news values, and the possible reasons for bias in reporting. Its conclusions were critical of the press as a whole, though it was also the Commission's view that there was no easy solution to its many difficulties.

Conclusions and implications for the future
572. We have given reasons why in our opinion the newspapers, with few exceptions, fail to supply the electorate with adequate materials for sound political judgements. This situation has arisen in part from the modern conception of news value. In part it also reflects the failure of the Press to keep pace with social requirements which grow steadily more exacting. The increased complexity of public affairs

and the growth of the reading public have created a need for public instruction on an entirely new scale without producing as yet either the corresponding demand or the corresponding supply. It is a peculiarity of a newspaper that it is produced by a profession grafted on to a highly competitive industry: whatever the ideals of the profession, they can be realised only within the conditions set by the industry....

574. The problem of bridging the gap between the rising standards of mental nutrition required for healthy citizenship in a modern democracy and the fare provided by the Press is not easily solved.... In a competitive industry, the more scrupulous are always in danger of being undercut by the less. When this situation occurs in industry, it can be, and often is, dealt with by legislation: alternatively, it is obviated by the establishment of a monopoly. The dangers which would attach to either these solutions in the case of the Press need no emphasis.

Royal Commission on the Press 1947–49 (Chairman: Sir W. D. Ross), *Report*, London: HMSO, Cmd 7700, June 1949, pp. 154–5.

4.4 Concentration of ownership in the industry: the view of the 1947–49 Commission

The Commission identified many factors which exacerbated the problems of the industry as it saw it. These included excessive competition, sensationalism, elements of political bias, an absence of diversity, and so on. However, it did not see the problem as simply one of concentration of ownership. Furthermore, it found no 'solutions' which were not without their own difficulties and drawbacks.

SUMMARY OF CONCLUSIONS AND RECOMMENDATIONS
What degree of concentration of ownership of newspapers, periodicals, and news agencies exists?

664. There is nothing approaching monopoly in the Press as a whole or with the single exception of the London financial daily, in any class of newspaper: nor is there in those classes of periodical which we have examined....

Is there a tendency towards further concentration of ownership?

670. Between 1921 and 1948 there has been a marked tendency

away from concentration of ownership in the national Press. We see no reason to expect a reversal of this tendency. In the provincial Press the trend was strongly towards concentration between 1921 and 1929: thereafter the trend was much less pronounced and in terms of the largest single newspaper chain was reversed. There is no reason to expect that the aggressive expansion of chain undertakings which characterised the earlier period will be resumed....

Is such concentration as exists on balance disadvantageous to the free expression of opinion or the accurate presentation of news?

672. The present degree of concentration of ownership ... is not so great as to prejudice the free expression of opinion or the accurate presentation of news or to be contrary to the best interests of the public. Newspaper chains are undesirable not in themselves, but only if they are so large and so few that they unduly limit the number and variety of voices speaking to the public through the Press. We should not be alarmed by any increase in the number of relatively small chains; but we should deplore any tendency on the part of the larger chains to expand....

674. The decrease in the number of newspapers, which is an aspect of concentration of ownership, has not been so great as to prejudice the public interest; but any further decrease in the number of national newspapers would be a matter for anxiety, and a decrease in the provincial morning newspapers would be a serious loss....

Do any other factors in the control, management, or ownership of the Press ... militate against the free expression of opinion and the accurate presentation of news? ...

677. ... The first requirement (see above) is satisfied in very different measure by different papers. A number of quality papers do fully or almost fully meet its demands. But all the popular papers and certain of the quality fall short of the standard achieved by the best, either through excessive partisanship or through distortion for the sake of news values....

678. ... the Press provides for a sufficient variety of political opinion but not for a sufficient variety of intellectual levels. The gap between the best of the quality papers and the general run of the popular Press is too wide, and the number of papers of an intermediate type is too small.

679. The causes of ... shortcomings [in the press] do not lie in any external influences upon the Press [other than those exerted by public demand]. The policy of the Press is dictated neither by the advertisers,

nor by the Government, nor by any outside financial interests. It is the policy of those who own and conduct the Press. Nor do the causes of the shortcomings lie in any particular form of ownership.

680. ... The failure of the Press to keep pace with the requirements of society is attributable largely to the plain fact that an industry that lives by the sale of its products must give the public what the public will buy. A newspaper cannot, therefore, raise its standard far above that of its public and may anticipate profit from lowering its standard in order to gain an advantage over a competitor. This tendency is not always resisted as firmly as the public interest requires. The Press does not do all it might to encourage its public to accept or demand material of higher quality.

How this freedom and accuracy [of the Press] may best be promoted

682. We do not see a solution to the problems we have indicated in major changes in the ownership and control of the industry. Free enterprise is a prerequisite of a free Press ...

683. Nor do we see the solution in any form of state control. We prefer to seek the means of maintaining the free expression of opinion and the greatest practicable accuracy in the presentation of news, and, generally, a proper relationship between the Press and society, primarily in the Press itself.

684. Accordingly *we recommend*:–

I. That the Press should establish a General Council of the Press ...

The objects of the General Council should be to safeguard the freedom of the Press; to encourage the growth of the sense of responsibility and public service amongst all engaged in the profession of journalism ...; and to further the efficiency of the profession and the well-being of those who practise it.

Royal Commission on the Press 1947–49 (Chairman: Sir W. D. Ross), *Report*, London: HMSO, Cmd 7700, June 1949, pp. 175–7.

4.5 The second post-war Royal Commission on the Press, 1961–62

The terms of reference of the second Royal Commission on the Press (1961–62) under the Chairmanship of Lord Shawcross took for granted the duties and responsibilities of the press which had been set out by its predecessor but it showed a growing concern about the longer-term survival of newspapers, particularly as it was set up immediately after a series of closures. The most dramatic of these was the demise of the *News Chronicle* in 1960, but there were other changes which raised concerns:

- the circulation of national dailies and Sundays had gone down from 38.5 million to 36.1 million between 1947 and 1960;
- although one new Sunday quality had been established since 1947 (the *Sunday Telegraph*), three popular Sundays had disappeared (*Dispatch*, *Graphic* and *Chronicle*);
- London evening papers and provincial Sunday papers and weeklies had declined in numbers.

251. Our terms of reference require us to consider whether the economic and financial factors affecting the production and sale of newspapers and periodicals tend to diminish their number or variety and the diversity of their ownership and control. In general their natural tendency is to do so. In distinguishing the particular economic factors which have this effect it is important to take account of those which make it difficult to start a new newspaper as well as those which put an established newspaper into difficulty. Since the report of the 1949 Commission only four daily or Sunday newspapers have been started against the seventeen which have perished.

A. COMPETITION

252. There can be little doubt that a most potent factor in diminishing the number and variety of publications is the distinctive character of the competition of one newspaper with another....

254. A number of witnesses – principally those concerned with the management of newspapers – were asked to tell us frankly why they thought the *News Chronicle* failed. Their answers were variations on the theme expressed by its own proprietors: that its formula and momentum were out of tune with the times with the result that its readership was both nondescript and comparatively small, and therefore unattractive to advertisers. It was suggested that the management had spent their resources unwisely: expenditure on new plant was never justified by the demand. We are bound to say that the majority of witnesses who expressed an opinion on the matter blamed the management of the newspaper for the result. It is no part

of our function to apportion responsibility in this matter, but we cannot escape the conclusion that the failure of the *News Chronicle* was not entirely the result of an inevitable law of newspaper economics; different and more consistent managerial and editorial policy might have saved this newspaper.

Royal Commission on the Press 1961–62 (Chairman: Lord Shawcross), *Report*, London: HMSO, Cmnd 1811, September 1962, pp. 80–1.

4.6 Solving the problems of the press: the 1961–62 Commission

The 1961–62 Commission looked at different aspects of newspaper production in order to work out possible remedies for the industry. It looked at the costs of production, cost of newsprint, the nature of advertising revenue, amongst other things, but came to no conclusion about these. Indeed, it warned against state intervention. In a separate chapter it looked, in detail, at the possible remedies that had been reported to it, and again it came out against them.

278. Although in our opinion the public interest is not being seriously injured by the present economic situation of the Press, the future effect of the various economic pressures must cause grave anxiety. Against the economic background, however, it is essential to keep constantly in mind the fact that, while legislative interference with market forces might conceivably check strong newspapers and bolster up weak ones, there is no way to success but through the quality of management and editorial direction. Legislation cannot produce these qualities. The question is whether it might mitigate the dangers to which those papers which lack inspired leadership are exposed. And those dangers are considerable.

PART IV. EXAMINATION OF POSSIBLE REMEDIES
CHAPTER 12. ECONOMIC REMEDIES
279. The following economic and financial remedies for the current difficulties of the Press which we have considered fall into two groups with entirely distinct objects. The first group was concerned with reducing the cost of production or at least alleviating the financial

problems of publications generally, while the possibilities in the second group were directed to tempering the forces of competition....

Conclusion

313. The remedies which we have discussed ... represent the major approaches to the problem. We are all forced to the conclusion – which we regret because of our clear realisation of the dangers which exist – that there is no acceptable legislative or fiscal way of regulating the competitive and economic forces so as to ensure a sufficient diversity of newspapers. The only hope of the weaker newspapers is to secure – as some have done in the past – managers and editors of such enterprise and originality as will enable these publications to overcome the economic forces affecting them.

Royal Commission on the Press 1961–62 (Chairman: Lord Shawcross), *Report*, London: HMSO, Cmnd 1811, September 1962, pp. 89, 99.

4.7 One possible scheme to help the press: the 1961–62 Commission

Numerous schemes were presented to the Commission. All, as the above extract shows, were rejected. One of these is highlighted below.

The Plan proposed by Mr. Kaldor and Mr. Neild

293. The object of another scheme ... was not to divert advertising away from the strong newspapers – although that might be one result of the plan – but to improve the competitive position of the smaller circulation newspapers by reducing the advantages which, in the present economic structure of the industry, spring simply from large circulations. Mr. Kaldor and Mr. Neild pointed to the great benefits enjoyed by newspapers which succeed in gaining an initial lead in circulation over their rivals and which can then exploit their extra profits by employing forms of competition which, the authors considered, bear little relation to the real needs of readers. If the advantages of mere size of circulations were removed, the success of a newspaper would depend on its true merit as a vehicle for news and not on its ability to employ what the authors regard as sensational and extravagant devices to attract readers. In their view, the result of the present

market forces was to deprive a substantial number of readers of the kind of newspaper which really suits their needs.

294. [The authors] proposed a remedy in the form of a levy on advertising revenue which would be imposed at a percentage rate which would rise with the newspaper's circulation. The proceeds would be distributed proportionately to circulation but the excess of any newspaper's circulation over a certain figure (for example two million copies a day) would be ignored. There would be one such equalisation pool for all daily morning newspapers and one for Sunday newspapers ...

Royal Commission on the Press 1961–62 (Chairman: Lord Shawcross), *Report*, London: HMSO, Cmnd 1811, September 1962, p. 93.

4.8 The recommendations of the 1961–62 Commission

On the general problems of the press, the Commission made no specific recommendations. But on three matters, the Commission did make recommendations. First, it suggested that newspaper groups should make public more information about their ownership of undertakings; second, it recommended that the General Council for the Press be set up in line with the 1949 recommendations (see pp. 135–6 above); and third, it proposed that mergers be considered by a Press Amalgamations Court. With respect to action to deal with the concentration of ownership, the Commission was ambivalent.

18. Taking all dailies together, it is clear that the extent of concentration has been substantially increased since the report of the 1949 Commission. The three leading undertakings controlled sixty-seven per cent. of the total circulation in 1961 against forty-five per cent. in 1948, ...

19. With Sunday newspapers also, there has been a substantial increase in the extent of concentration, as the three leading undertakings controlled eighty-four per cent. of the circulation in 1961 against sixty-one per cent. in 1948....

20. The position may perhaps best be summed up in terms of the aggregate number of copies, taking daily and Sunday newspapers

together, sold in each week of seven days by the undertakings with the biggest circulations. On this basis the position is as follows: –

All daily and Sunday Newspapers

1948 Undertaking	Per cent of circ.	1961 Undertaking	Per cent of circ.
Beaverbrook Newspapers	16	Daily Mirror group	27
Associated Newspapers	14	Associated Newspapers	19
Kemsley Newspapers	13	Beaverbrook Newspapers	19
Top Three	43	Top Three	65

247. The advantages (and possible disadvantages) of a diversification of interests by Press undertakings do not differ in any fundamental respect from those which accrue to all concerns in spreading their interests and their risks: a development of the post-war period which has been seen in a large number of industries besides the Press....

249. In most instances a publication stands or falls on its own merits, whether it is one of a number under common ownership or not: it will survive only if it is profitable, or likely to become profitable within a reasonable period without involving disproportionate losses in the meantime. In a multiple undertaking, however, a publication may survive even though the accounts show it as unprofitable, if the loss is less than the amount of additional overheads which would fall on other publications if it were discontinued. Or it may be continued if it makes some other contribution to the undertaking: for example, its existence may fend off competition that would otherwise hurt its companions. Moreover, the resources open to a strong multiple undertaking may enable a weak publication to be supported and improved with a view to long-term results, if policy so suggests. On the other hand multiple ownership may also lead to the death of the profitable publication if it is expected that as a result the profits of the whole undertaking will be increased through a greater concentration of readers or advertisers in its remaining publications. Moreover the will to keep a publication alive may be much weaker when it is a relatively unimportant member of a multiple undertaking than it is when a publication provides the sole livelihood of the proprietor and staff of a small undertaking.

250. To sum up: a certain amount of multiple ownership in the Press contributes, on balance, to the maintenance of the number and

variety of newspapers and periodicals. Strong units are essential to a healthy Press, and strength frequently rests upon multiple ownership. How far this multiple ownership can be carried without harming the public interest is another matter.

Royal Commission on the Press 1961–62 (Chairman: Lord Shawcross), *Report*, London: HMSO, Cmnd 1811, September 1962, pp. 13–15, 79–80.

4.9 The Economic Intelligence Unit report and its analysis of the industry

The Economist Intelligence Unit (EIU) sought to provide information for the industry which would lead to an 'increased efficiency in the publication and production of national newspapers'. Although the report itself makes no recommendations, the need for urgent action was underlined by Lord Devlin in his introduction to the report.

If the report is right greater efficiency is not the complete answer. The forecast is that before this decade ends, if present trends continue, three more national dailies and one more national Sunday will have gone. They will not be swallowed up by tycoons anxious to foist their own brands of politics on increasing masses. There are no such people. This report destroys utterly the idea that newspapers can be kept forcibly alive by anti-monopoly legislation. If these newspapers die ... here is what their death certificates will say. A change in the reading habits of the public caused a decline in overall circulation – 10% in dailies in eight years and 23% in Sundays – and this chronic weakness was aggravated to fatality by an economic depression hitting the advertising revenue on which these newspapers, sold by the standards of other countries too cheaply, had become dependent.

Economist Intelligence Unit, *The National Newspaper Industry: A Survey*, London: EIU, 1966, Introduction by Lord Devlin, p. 2.

Proprietorial control as such is not necessarily inimical to the interests of the industry. It is the way that it is exercised in certain companies that has repercussions on the quality of management and on the day to day method of operation within those companies.

In some organisations the essential drive and interest from the top is directed solely towards the editorial function, in others the proprietor has delegated functional responsibility but has retained the authority which is necessary to let those functions operate efficiently.

Some proprietors appear to have little interest in modern management methods and techniques yet retain almost absolute authority over the organisation. This tends to stifle the initiative of the other members of the management team and indirectly has an effect on the calibre of management.

... it is difficult to see how an efficient and prosperous industry can be achieved unless all proprietors become as interested in running an efficient *business*, as they are in producing a good newspaper, and are prepared to co-operate with each other towards that end.

There are ... companies, where there is little or no sophisticated financial control, where top management functions are imprecisely defined and where there is little interest in long term planning or training for the future....

A major defect in most companies is the absence of a proper marketing function to act as a catalyst for the advertisement and circulation departments; ...

The problems of editorial management are not in our opinion taken seriously enough by most parts of the industry.... In many companies communications between different sides of the business are poor.... In several companies middle managers complained that they were uncertain about company policy in a number of respects and the implications of new appointments were not made clear....

Two things stand out in the Newspaper industry as being likely to impede progress in the adoption of new techniques and more efficient practices. First there is the fact that sons have followed fathers into the trade for many years so that very little is known about conditions in other industries.... Secondly, there is a high proportion of elderly men ... [whose ideas have] become rigid. A few younger men deride the fact that they are doing a job in precisely the same way as their grandfathers. These young men are, however, in a minority, and tend to believe that there is no prospect of change....

Newspaper workers often fail to realise that their industry is almost unique in the degree to which control of labour is in the hands of the Unions. The fact that quite large numbers of men spend a large proportion of their working lives negotiating, taking part in deputations and meetings among themselves is not thought to be at all unusual.

There is no doubt that many people in the industry are acutely aware of its shortcomings. They are nevertheless prepared to tolerate the situation, either because it pays them to do so or because they feel there is nothing they can do to change things....

[In the production area]

(i) Little use is made of normal production engineering, planning and control techniques in the industry, and few organisations are large enough to recruit specialists of high calibre.

(ii) Although new equipment is at times installed, the evaluation of new equipment and techniques often appears to be carried out in a haphazard manner. Where new equipment is installed it is not always used to its full effectiveness due to difficulties in agreeing manning standards.

(iii) Manning standards are usually set by horse trading, and often bear little relationship to the needs of the job. This leads to anomalies in work load and rewards between departments and sections.

(iv) The present wage structure is a jungle, and the basic wage bears no relationship to the take home pay. This leads to continual demands for extras of all kinds, and is a basic cause of friction and unrest.

Economist Intelligence Unit, *The National Newspaper Industry: A Survey*, London: EIU, 1966, pp. 53–5, 93–4, Conclusions p. 60.

4.10   The third Royal Commission on the Press, 1974–77

By the time the third Royal Commission on the Press was established in 1974, the main concerns about the industry had been well rehearsed. There were fears about further closures, concerns about an inefficient industry, concerns about its long-term survival, concerns about change, concerns about a narrowing of choice. In one sense, then, the 1974–77 Commission appeared to be treading a well-worn path.

[The Commission's task was] 'to inquire into the factors affecting the maintenance of the independence, diversity and editorial standards of newspapers and periodicals, and the public's freedom of choice of newspapers and periodicals, nationally, regionally and locally, with particular reference to:

(a) the economics of newspaper and periodical publishing and distribution;

(b) the interaction of newspapers and periodical interests held by the companies concerned with their other interest and holdings, within and outside the communications industry;

(c) management and labour practices and relations in the newspaper and periodical industry;

(d) conditions and security of employment in the newspaper and periodical industry;

(e) the distribution and concentration of ownership of the newspaper and periodical industry, and the adequacy of existing law in relation thereto;

(f) the responsibilities, constitution and funding of the Press Council; and to make recommendations' ...

3.1 ... There are nine national daily and seven national Sunday newspapers, one fewer in both categories than in 1961 ...

3.2 Two titles have closed since 1961. The *Sunday Citizen* ... ceased publication in 1967, and the *Daily Sketch* merged with the *Daily Mail* in 1971. In a further change, the *Daily Herald* became the *Sun* ... it was acquired in 1969 by what is now News International.

3.3 Other changes ... are that *The Guardian* and *The Financial Times* have become firmly established as nationals. Three newspapers launched and continue to publish colour supplements ...

3.9 ... In England and Wales there are now [in 1977] only 12 provincial morning papers as against 18 in 1948.... There are no provincial morning newspapers in South East England, nor since the closure of the *Nottingham Guardian Journal* in 1973, in the East Midlands. There is ... a provincial morning newspaper in every other main geographical region, and in each of the major conurbations except Manchester.

3.10 ... There are 77 evening newspapers in the United Kingdom outside London. Nine have closed since 1961, eight of these were in direct competition with another in the same town. With the exception of London, no town in the United Kingdom now has more than one evening newspaper....

Royal Commission on the Press 1974–77 (Chairman: O. R. McGregor), *Final Report*, London: HMSO, Cmnd 6810, July 1977, pp. xix, 12–14.

4.11 The standard by which the press should be judged (1974–77)

The 1974–77 Royal Commission worked with a much broadened definition of the place of the press in the turbulent 1970s. But was this fundamentally different from the first post-war Commission's work?

2.2 Freedom of the press carries different meanings for different people. Some emphasise the freedom of proprietors to market their publications, others the freedom of individuals, whether professional journalist or not, to address the public through the press; still others stress the freedom of editors to decide what shall be published. These are all elements in the right to freedom of expression. But proprietors, contributors and editors must accept the limits to free expression set by the need to reconcile claims which may often conflict. The public, too, asserts a right to accurate information and fair comment which, in turn, has to be balanced against the claims both of national security and of individuals to safeguards for their reputation and privacy except when these are overridden by the public interest. But the public interest does not reside in whatever the public may happen to find interesting, and the press must be careful not to perpetrate abuses and call them freedom. Freedom of the press cannot be absolute. There must be boundaries to it and realistic discussion concerns where those boundaries ought to be set.

2.3 We define freedom of the press as that degree of freedom from restraint which is essential to enable proprietors, editors and journalists to advance the public interest by publishing the facts and opinions without which a democratic electorate cannot make responsible judgements. However, some parts of the press are more subject to economic than to other forms of restraint. Anyone is free to start a daily national newspaper, but few can afford even to contemplate the prospect. Among the questions that we have to consider are whether the public can obtain the information and opinions it needs in this democracy without a range of diverse newspapers as wide as or wider than at present available, and whether the public interest in diversity may not be so great as to justify removing or reducing financial constraints by some form of subsidy....

2.12 There is thus a consensus, shared by almost all of those who gave evidence to us, that the press should neither be subject to state control nor left entirely to the unregulated forces of the market. We share that general accord, and much of our report is devoted to drawing out its implications....

Measuring Press Performance

10.1 Our definition of freedom of the press ... stresses the need for it to be free to perform those functions which are important in a democracy.... the functions of the press [meet] the requirements of readers for news, information and entertainment, helping them to plan their daily lives, to buy or sell their goods and to enjoy their leisure. At [another] level, it provides a forum for debate about cultural, social and political issues of the day, or scrutinises the activities of governmental and private organisations. Each of these functions has to be judged by different standards as well as by such professional criteria as speed, originality, style and layout. Moreover, the pressures which the nature of the market imposes upon journalists are important too....

10.3 Nevertheless, the standards of truth, accuracy and fairness can be applied from whatever standpoint the press is being judged. Although these may involve subjective judgements and sometimes be difficult to apply in detail, they must be met in any piece of journalism. There are also certain forms of behaviour in collecting information which should be regarded as intolerable.

Royal Commission on the Press 1974–77 (Chairman: O. R. McGregor), *Final Report*, London: HMSO, Cmnd 6810, July 1977, pp. 8–9, 75–6.

4.12 The measure of concentration in the national press, 1977

The 1974–77 Royal Commission did not produce tables of the sort that highlighted levels of concentration across the industry (see 4.8 above). It was, nevertheless, aware of the changing nature of concentration, just as it was aware of the changing nature of ownership itself. Since then, there have been significant changes in the ownership of newspapers and these will undoubtedly continue in the industry as newspapers compete fiercely with each other for a share of the readership (see 4.22).

4.4 Of the 10 companies controlling national newspapers, six (Reed International, S Pearson and Son, The Thomson Organisation, News International, Associated Newspapers Group and Atlantic Richfield) have substantial interests outside newspaper and periodical publishing. The Guardian and Manchester Evening News Limited also publishes provincial newspapers. By contrast, the Daily Telegraph Limited and Beaverbrook Newspapers are almost entirely confined to publishing national newspapers. However, more than one-third of the non-voting shares of Beaverbrook Newspapers is now owned by Cavenham, a holding company with many subsidiaries which are mainly food suppliers and retailers. It is itself a subsidiary company of Générale Occidentale, a French company with activities in banking and financial services. The Morning Star Co-operative Society is solely concerned with newspaper publishing.

4.5 Since the purchase of The Observer Limited by Atlantic Richfield, three of the ten national newspaper companies are ultimately controlled from outside the country. People from other countries have often become owners of British newspapers....

CONCENTRATION OF OWNERSHIP
Measure of concentration
4.16 The 1961–2 Royal Commission pointed out that concentration of ownership in the newspaper and periodical publishing industry cannot be measured by any single index. The usual measures are either the number of titles or the circulation controlled by one or a given number of companies as a proportion of the total. In general, we agree ... in using circulation as the better measure of the extent to which the supply of news and opinion is controlled, actually or potentially, by a few proprietors.

National Newspapers
4.17 So far as the national newspaper industry is concerned, we consider concentration of ownership of popular and of quality newspapers separately. Popular newspapers have a much larger total circulation than the qualities and it would be misleading to lump

them together when considering concentration of ownership. No proprietor publishes both a popular and a quality newspaper.

4.18 The proportionate share of total weekly sales achieved by three of the publishers of popular national daily and Sunday newspapers has changed markedly since 1961. Associated Newspapers Group's share of total weekly sales has almost halved to nearly 12% in 1976.... Daily Mirror Newspapers and Sunday Pictorial Newspapers held the largest share in 1961 and Reed International still does, although it has fallen from 44% in 1961 to 35% in 1976.... News International's share of total popular weekly sales is now just over 30%.

4.19 Among the quality nationals, The Daily Telegraph Limited still leads with 56% of total weekly sales. The major change has been that The Thomson Organisation, which already owned *The Sunday Times*, acquired The Times Publishing Company in 1966. This, together with an increase in the circulation of *The Sunday Times*, has increased The Thomson Organisation's share from 7% in 1961 to 20% in 1976....

4.38 Four ... companies, Atlantic Richfield, Reed International, BET and S. Pearson and Son, receive a larger income from their other activities than from newspaper and periodical publishing and have substantial overseas interests. Newspaper and periodical publishing accounted for less than 3% of BET's turnover in 1975. S. Pearson and Son's main activities, apart from newspaper and book publishing, are merchant banking and industrial interests. Activities other than newspaper and periodical publishing accounted for over three-quarters of the company's income in 1975....

4.40 All of these companies have since 1961 significantly expanded both the areas of their activity and the diversity of their holdings. In this growth, these companies have done no more than follow the general trend in British industry. However, the joint ownership of newspapers and periodicals and other interests has major implications ...

Royal Commission on the Press 1974–77 (Chairman: O. R. McGregor), *Final Report*, London: HMSO, Cmnd 6810, July 1977, pp. 22, 24–5, 29.

4.13 Helping the industry: the minority view

The final report did not favour any particular form of state intervention. There were two dissenting voices – Messrs Basnett and Goodman – who felt that some state action was not only necessary and desirable but also urgently needed. Their idea, which was only sketched in the report, included the setting up of a National Printing Corporation to aid the printing of newspapers, and the introduction of a launch fund to help establish new titles. The emphasis was on creating diversity within both a politically restricted spectrum of opinion and a stark divide between tabloids and broadsheets.

2. ... we do not believe [the majority view] deals with sufficient strength and urgency with the dangers facing the British Press....

3. Nor is it enough to advocate ... reforms in the financial, technological and manpower structure of the industry vital though they are. Neither is it enough merely to consider improving the industrial relations atmosphere with changes in the institutional framework of management/labour relations. These are of course areas of great importance but they ought to be seen as part of a wider problem which is: the nature and character of the press. We believe the British press is not as bad as many of its critics claim, but we also believe it is still far from good enough to cope with the variety of social, economic and cultural challenges which our society is now experiencing and which, in our view, it will face with increasing tensions during the next decade....

6. Our general stand is based on the view that market pressures now increasingly imposing themselves on the national press constitute a serious impediment to existing diversity, and an even greater one to hopes of expanding upon that diversity.... in our view what these pressures are also doing is to diminish the stature of much that is excellent in popular journalism, and to emphasise and highlight that which is questionable if not objectionable and even obscene....

7. Indeed, in the analysis of the problem we find ourselves supported by the majority report which states, 'we have no doubt that there is a gap in political terms which could be filled with advantage. However, no one knows whether the readership of such a paper would enable it to survive commercially'.

8. We are in agreement with that analysis. Where we depart from

the majority is that they are not prepared to suggest measures which would at least try to overcome these commercial obstacles.

D. Basnett and G. Goodman, Minority Report, in Royal Commission on the Press 1974–77 (Chairman: O. R. McGregor), *Final Report*, London: HMSO, Cmnd 6810, July 1977, pp. 241, 242.

4.14 The 1974–77 Royal Commission report and its inconsistencies

> The Commission was heavily criticised by those who felt that the diversity of the press was so restricted that radical, 'left-wing' views were not only under-represented but also vilified. Moreover, given the cost of establishing newspapers, the imbalance of political opinion would never be redressed. Many years later, Lord McCarthy did undertake a study of the possibility of establishing a 'labour movement' news-paper for the Trades Union Congress in which he concluded that there was a potential 'hard core' readership of 300,000 (1983: 44).

Underlying the objection of the ... Commission to selective or ongoing public funding of the press is the belief that the market mechanism is essentially neutral, while public intervention is potentially manipulative. This belief is reflected in the double standards that are consistently applied in the McGregor Report. Public agencies are forced to make 'invidious' choices, whereas private agencies merely take decisions. Selection by a public body is defined as an act of censorship, yet market allocation is assumed to be neutral. Redistributive schemes imposed by a public agency can never be 'objective'; the same problem of 'objectivity' does not arise in the free market. The trouble with redistributive schemes is that they have 'identifiable consequences' and therefore fall within the political arena; the existing pattern of market distribution does not need to be identified, however, because it is impersonal and outside the political arena.

... In short, objection is raised to selective public subsidies on the grounds that they could be discretionary, could make the difference between life and death of individual papers, and could be fixed in a

way that gives more help to papers supporting one political party
than to another. The fact that advertising subsidies are discretionary,
do make the difference between life and death for some papers, and
do give more help to papers supporting one political party than
another is accepted as the natural – and politically neutral – order of
things.

J. Curran, 'Introduction', in J. Curran (ed.), *The British Press: A
Manifesto*, London: Macmillan, 1978, pp. 3–4.

4.15   Why newspapers die

Newspaper closures were always a cause of concern, but why
did newspapers cease publication (see extract 4.5)? One
insight into the problems of the industry was provided by
Michael Mander in a brief review of newspaper economics
from the 1930s to the 1970s.

By the mid-fifties those newspapers that had gathered for themselves
– by skill, chance or intuition – readerships that were either very big
or small but specialised were the ones that prospered. The rest died.
They varied in circulation from the *Empire News* – 2.1 million – to
Reynolds News at 300 000. But they had one thing in common – no
defined and saleable advertisement market (See Figure 7.1).

Figure 7.1 shows the last reported position of those national newspapers that have sunk since 1955, as well as the current plots of the
survivors. The axes are circulation and ABC1 share of profile. The
vulnerability of the *Express* and *Mail* are highlighted; they have been
in the past neither big enough to challenge the advertisement markets
of the populars, nor specialised enough to challenge the qualities....

The key question is whether a big enough advertisement market
exists, or can be persuaded to exist, to match their circumstances; or
whether through editorial change they can alter the nature and size of
their readership enough to move into the already strong competitive
markets of the populars or the qualities.

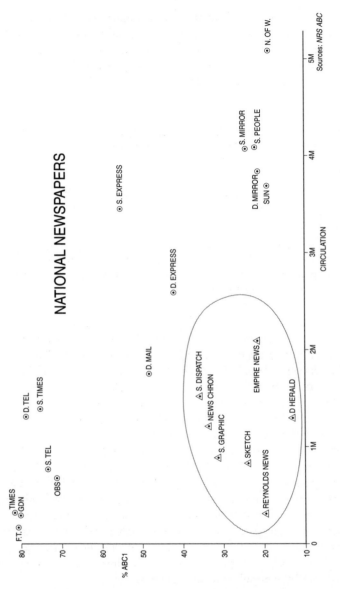

M. Mander, 'The integration of advertising and circulation sales policies', in H. Henry, *Behind the Headlines: The Business of the British Press. Readings in the Economics of the Press*, London: Associated Business Press, 1978, p. 79.

4.16   The problems of the press: old-fashioned practices and control by labour unions

In the 1960s and 1970s the newspaper industry faced considerable difficulties – difficulties which, in the 1990s, are hard to imagine (see 4.9). The next two extracts give a flavour of the period. From these extracts one can also gain an insight into the sorts of solutions being proposed to deal with the problems of the industry, namely, inefficiency, over-manning, old-techniques, and control by the labour unions.

In newspapers ... text was set on a linotype machine, differing little from the iron comp of the 1890s.... The operator sits at a wide keyboard on which 90 keys are organised in three banks, reflecting the lower and upper case of hand setting, and an additional alphabet of 'small capitals' together with digits and symbols. He also has a choice of magazines containing different type styles or sizes. Each keystroke he makes releases a small brass matrix, a tiny hollow mould of a single letter of the alphabet, from the overhead magazine. The matrices slide, one at a time, down a shute in response to the operator's keystrokes collecting in an assembler where they may be read as a line. The linotype has a clever device of wedge-shaped spacebands that spread out the words to form a tight line according to the required width (measure), making possible a straight right-hand edge to the column text (justification). The operator must make a decision at the end of each line as to when to stop adding characters and whether to break a word, running it over to the next line (hyphenation). The collected matrices are then 'sent away' by pressing a lever. Molten metal is forced into the faces of the characters resulting in a solid slug or 'line o' type' about one inch high, which is ejected onto a waiting tray (galley). Here the lines, still hot to the touch, assemble, as the operator taps away, into columns of text. The used matrices are mechanically lifted to the top of the machine where, by a system of coded notches cut in the base of each one, they are distributed back, each into its appropriate channel of the magazine, to await re-use....

We tend to think of technological revolutions as being expressed only in machinery. But they are also revolutions in management. It is not only the formal agreement over wages and hours of work that concerns the employer, but how hard and well the employee works. The pace of work, the division of labour, who gives the orders, the quality of the product, safety, all may become subjects of struggle between the employer and the worker.... Photocomposition and computer technology in printing cannot be seen as standing alone; they are part of a politics of control.

C. Cockburn, *Brothers: Male Dominance and Technological Change*, London: Pluto Press, 1984, pp. 47–8, 88–9.

4.17 Newspaper shut-downs and loss of print runs

The 'politics of control' is an apt phrase to describe the nature of industrial relations (and related issues) in Fleet Street in the 1960s and 1970s. The tradition in Fleet Street had been for newspaper owners to pay their way out of trouble and to work towards success by paying more than average wages. For their part, unions – extending a tradition going back to the early days of the print industry – exerted control over all aspects of production. With this state of affairs, employers' attempts to exert control over the industry were bound to be vehemently resisted. The question, often posed in the 1960s and 1970s, was whether events would precipitate the intro-duction of new technology and on whose terms.

In 1978 *The Times* was shut down for a whole year. The subsequent return to work had made little difference to rela-tions within *The Times*, and within Fleet Street more gener-ally. If there was disruption before the shut-down, there was also disruption after. According to Harold Evans, then editor of the *Sunday Times*, 3.5 million copies of the *Sunday Times* had been lost in April 1980 and by November the number of copies lost had tripled. The paper had become 'The Sunday Sometimes'.

By May [1980] a drearily familiar pattern of lost copies of *The Sun-day Times* had reasserted itself. The newspaper had failed to achieve its full print run on thirteen of the first nineteen issues of 1980, and only one issue, that of 3 February, had been distributed in full and on time. The company had lost £1,209,000 from this alone – £385,000 from copies that could not be sold because they were not printed, and the rest in cash that had to be paid in rebates to advertisers who failed to reach all the readers they had paid for. One manager wrote plaintively to Mander: 'It is essential that the danger now be recognised for what it really is: a threat to the very future of *The Sunday Times*.'

E. Jacobs, *Stop Press: The Inside Story of the Times Dispute*, London: Andre Deutsch, 1980, p. 151.

4.18   How to help the industry: the view of the 1961–62 Royal Commission

Although significant financial savings could be achieved in the industry – the Daily Mirror Group estimated that it could do with 40 per cent fewer staff 'in the machine rooms, publishing rooms and transport sections' (Cmnd 1811, September 1962, p. 31, para. 75) – these were not the only answer to all its problems. In later years, however, many were to see savings in production through computerisation and other 'new technologies' as the principal solution to the industry's difficulties.

261. ... a general reduction in labour costs or a general improvement in efficiency of production would not in the long term have assisted newspapers which have fallen behind in the race with their immediate rivals. The level of earnings and the degree of efficiency do however vary, especially between the national and provincial newspapers. Hence the scope for economies varies also. An improvement in efficiency largely concentrated in national newspapers (where the scope for improvement is greatest) would, of course, strengthen their competitive position as against that of provincial mornings.

262. If a proprietor is able by some means to secure an increase in efficiency which his rivals cannot match, he will, of course, derive full competitive advantage from it; or at least it may help him to offset any competitive disadvantage he may suffer in another respect. This goes some way to explain how provincial mornings manage to survive in competition with the nationals despite a much smaller circulation....

Royal Commission on the Press 1961–62 (Chairman: Lord Shawcross), *Report*, London: HMSO, Cmnd 1811, September 1962, p. 83.

4.19   How to help the industry: the National Board for Prices and Incomes, 1967

The problems of inefficient production and cost reductions in a highly competitive industry were also addressed in two National Board for Prices and Incomes reports on the newspaper industry (Cmnd 3435, October 1967; Cmnd 4277, February 1970). Both reports included general analyses of the state of the industry. The 1967 report also noted that one of the concerns about government intervention to help the industry was that any act of intervention, however benevolent, could be discriminatory (p. 17, para. 52).

36. ... the financial situation of the newspaper industry is due to three factors. These are: first, the nature of competition within the industry which has caused some newspapers to be highly profitable while others make heavy losses ...; secondly, the advent of commercial television which has taken revenue which might otherwise have gone to the press; thirdly, on the cost side the nature of competition has made for excessive costs, these being particularly marked in the field of manpower.

37. In the light of the general financial position of the industry it would be foolish to pretend that there will not be further contraction [in the industry].... in spite of all the uncertainties we are of the opinion that, unless present trends can be changed, one or more of the existing newspapers will eventually be forced to close down....

49. Cost reduction in this industry must inevitably be concerned with the problem of manpower.... This is a problem which needs to be tackled urgently and systematically. Clearly it is the responsibility of the industry, in conjunction with the trade unions, to determine how any resulting redundancies should be dealt with. But in the light of the scale of the problem we consider that the Government should make it its own responsibility to mitigate the consequences.... If, on the other hand, the industry were to seek to evade the cost problem by raising prices, we would not regard the Government as in duty bound to bear the same degree of responsibility.

50. ... We are of the opinion that the State should not consider any act of relief for the industry – beyond the help we have suggested to cope with the problem of redundancy – until it is satisfied that the industry's management is adequately dealing with those difficulties

which are primarily its own responsibility. Indeed it would be fair to add that the industry has expressed opposition to any act of Government intervention.

National Board for Prices and Incomes, *Costs and Revenue of National Daily Newspapers*, Report No. 43, London: HMSO, Cmnd 3435, 1967, pp. 2, 11–12, 16–17.

4.20   How to help the industry: forcing the pace of change

The difficulties experienced by the *Sunday Times* (see 4.17) were symptomatic of the state of affairs in the industry. Many saw the introduction of new technology and computerisation as a way of reducing not only labour power but also its power within newspaper publishing. Computerisation eliminated many of the jobs which Cynthia Cockburn had so vividly described (see 4.16).

But the unions fought hard against the introduction of new machinery. However, with Margaret Thatcher in government, and a new legislative agenda to deal with the unions, the balance of power shifted towards the proprietors. One thing which paved the way for 'new technology' was legislation which curbed the powers of the trade unions in industrial disputes. Both of these were in evidence during the early 1980s when Eddie Shah rejected the closed shop agreements – the traditional method by which print unions controlled printing plants – in his new typesetting subsidiary in Bury for his Messenger group of newspapers. After a long and bitter struggle with mass pickets and organised police action, in the form of the Tactical Aid Group, the unions truly lost the battle.

Most of the [2,000] pickets were stunned by the efficiency and ruthlessness of the police-clearing operation and started to hurry away.... It had been one of those rare, but uncomfortable, reminders that even in a mature democracy the struggle for industrial power can still involve a literal battle, and that the law remains ultimately underpinned by physical force....

At 4.45 in the morning, the vans finally screeched out of the plant with their load of weekly papers. Only a few die-hards were left to impotently shout 'scab'. It was the end of an era in trade union history, an end too for the effective use of a tactic that for the past ten years had come to represent the high watermark of trade union power. Tony Burke, the NGA Stockport branch president, admitted: 'Flying pickets were born at Saltley Gate and died at Warrington.' As the pickets, police and Messenger staff stumbled wearily home to catch a few hours' sleep, most people sensed it was the beginning of the end of the Messenger dispute. What they could not have predicted was that Winwick Quay had become the symbolic birthplace of a project which two-and-a-half years later was to help transform the national newspaper industry and directly inspire Rupert Murdoch's Wapping escapade.

D. Goodhart and P. Wintour, *Eddie Shah and the Newspaper Revolution*, London: Coronet, 1986, pp. 4, 12–13.

4.21 'The end of the street': to Wapping and Canary Wharf

The last formal meeting between the unions and Rupert Murdoch was held on 23 January 1986. It took place against a background of mounting tension. Murdoch had, only ten days before, 'given six months notice to terminate union agreements covering 5,500 production workers at the News Group and Times Newspapers' (Melvern, 1986: 2). By the 1990s, Fleet Street had lost all the national titles as they transferred to such places as Canary Wharf in East London.

Wapping [the site of his new printing plant in the East End of London] was all that the union leaders wanted to talk about that day: Murdoch's new, purpose-built plant in London's dockland, and the *London Post*, the newspaper he said he intended printing there. The £100 million newspaper factory was uppermost in the mind of every person in that room. Its very appearance was startling. It was a fortress, ringed with razor wire in huge coils, fenced with steel and constantly scanned by shifting eyes of closed-circuit cameras. It was built to be picket-proof....

This last meeting failed to avert the dispute. The next day, 5,500 print workers went on strike. It was Friday, 24th January 1986, and it was the end of the Street.

Television and the press since 1945

L. Melvern, *The End of the Street*, London: Methuen, 1986, pp. 3, 248.

4.22 Increased competition: the newspaper price war and circulation

The introduction of computerisation and the 'end of Fleet Street' saw a short period in which some new titles sprung up: the *Sunday Correspondent*, the *London Daily News*, *Today*, and *The Independent* amongst others. Of these, only *The Independent* managed to survive into adolescence. *Today*, for example, was swallowed up by News International in 1986 and then shut down in 1995.

In 1993 Rupert Murdoch launched a price war in the newspaper market. The cover price of *The Times* was cut from 45p to 30p on week-days. The loss of revenue for News International was thought to be £17 million over the year. There were also price cuts for *The Sun*. The effect of these price reductions was to increase the circulation of *The Times*, maintain that of *The Sun* and threaten the survival of one particular broadsheet, *The Independent*. It also made everyone in the industry conscious of the fact that the demand for newspapers was also price sensitive.

Circulation of national daily and sunday newspapers, 1947–1997 ('000s)

	1947	1961	1976	1987	1997
Daily Telegraph (1855)	1,015	1,248	1,308	1,147	1,082
The Times (1785)	268	253	310	442	783
The Guardian (1821)	*126	245	306	494	389
Financial Times (1888)	*71	132	174	280	342
The Independent (1986)	–	–	–	293	227
Daily Mail (1896)	2,076	2,610	1,755	1,759	2,190
Daily Express (1900)	3,855	4,328	2,594	1,697	1,136
Daily Herald (*The Sun* from 1964)	2,134	1,394	3,708	3,993	3,678
News Chronicle (1930)	1,623	†	–	–	–
Daily Worker (*Morning Star* from 1966)	118	60	‡	–	–

160

Daily Graphic (later *Sketch*) (1908)	772	981	§	–	–
Daily Mirror (1903)	3,702	4,561	3,851	3,123	2,211
Today (1986)	–	–	–	533	#
Daily Star (1978)	–	–	–	1,289	670

* The 1947–49 Royal Commission did not treat either of these newspapers as 'national' qualities.
† Absorbed by the *Daily Mail* in 1960.
‡ Not known.
§ Merged with *Daily Mail* in 1971.
# Shut down in 1995.

	1947	1961	1976	1988	1997
Sunday Telegraph (1961)		688	759	693	870
Sunday Times (1822)	568	967	1,382	1,314	1,304
The Observer (1791)	384	715	670	722	407
Independent on Sunday (1990)	–	–	–	–	267
News of the World (1843)	7,890	6,643	5,138	5,360	4,303
Reynolds News (1850) / *Sunday Citizen*	720	310	*	–	–
Sunday Express (1918)	2,577	4,457	3,451	2,033	1,046
Sunday Chronicle (1855)	1,178	†	–	–	–
Sunday Dispatch (1801)	2,061	‡	–	–	–
Sunday Pictorial / *Sunday Mirror* (1915)	4,006	5,306	#4,101	2,953	2,102
Sunday Graphic (1915)	1,185	§	–	–	–
The People (1881)	4,670	5,450	4,094	2,743	1,827
Mail on Sunday (1982)	–	–	–	1,919	2,151

* Shut down in 1967.
† Shut down in 1955.
‡ Shut down in 1961.
# With *Mirror*.
§ Shut down in 1960.

Sources: Figures derived from Royal Commissions on the Press 1947–49, 1961–62, 1974–77; C. Seymour-Ure, *The British Press and Broadcasting since 1945*, Oxford: Blackwell, 1991; *The Guardian*, 1997.

4.23 'Tabloidisation', or the changing face of newspapers

From the late 1980s, newspapers, and especially broadsheet newspapers, began to change quite significantly. One of the more obvious changes was the addition of supplements, but there was another change which was as dramatic. Newspapers redesigned themselves in such a way that their front pages – and their other pages – began to change substantially. Fewer stories were carried on their front pages, for example, and often those stories would be quite different from the sorts of stories which used to inhabit the front pages. One of the effects of that change was the demise of the 'parliamentary page' (see 3.25), though there were suspicions that the news agenda had also changed.

What is particularly interesting about the 1990s is that there appears to be little official concern about the long-term survival of the industry. Moreover, the danger of a further concentration of power in the industry or across the media industries, particularly under Rupert Murdoch, is appreciated but not acted upon. Tony Blair's closeness to Murdoch may have blunted the ability of the Labour government to act in these matters.

5

Aspects of press performance

THE POWER OF THE PROPRIETOR

How much power did newspaper proprietors exert over their newspapers? Were proprietors absentee landlords leaving the day-to-day running of the enterprise to appointed executives and editors?

5.1 Lord Beaverbrook as proprietor

Lord Beaverbrook's evidence to the 1947–49 Royal Commission showed that he dominated *The Express* newspaper but that the lack of attention given to the economic aspects of the paper was the result of a financial position which was not troublesome: 'there has always been plenty of money in the coffers, and therefore commercial things have come along rather easily for us' (Cmd 7416, March 1948, p. 157, para. 8710). The next two extracts expand on these points.

149. The present chairman of London Express Newspaper Ltd. ... said of Lord Beaverbrook:
'He never actually took any title; he has not been a director of the paper since 1920 but he was undoubtedly the paper. Lord Beaverbrook certainly formulated the policy and was a daily critic of the paper, took responsibility, advised and assisted. He was in daily contact, but he never had an office at any time in the building.'

Royal Commission on the Press 1947–49 (Chairman: Sir W. D. Ross), *Report*, London: HMSO, Cmd 7700, June 1949, p. 43.

8656. When you [Lord Beaverbrook] were more actively engaged in the conduct of the papers, was your main purpose (a) the commercial success of the paper, (b) the support of a particular political Party, or (c) the support of special political views which happened to be near to your own heart? – I ran the paper purely for propaganda, and with no other object.

8657. Propaganda, I [Chairman] take it, on particular issues, rather than general? – Particular issues, my own issue, the issue [Empire free trade] I have advocated all these years....

8660. Which would you think the more healthy set-up for the Press: papers run from the point of view of commercial success, or papers run to further a particular policy? – I do not think a paper is any good for propaganda unless you run it as a commercial success. That is essential, if you are to have a good propaganda instrument. My purpose originally was to set up a propaganda paper, and I have never departed from that purpose all through the years. But in order to make propaganda effective the paper had to be successful. No paper is any good at all for propaganda unless it has a thoroughly good financial position. So that we worked very hard to build-up a commercial position on that account, but never sacrificing propaganda; always making propaganda, but never in the news. Not only because it would not be a good thing to do, but because it would be bad commercially to turn out news as propaganda. That is the principle on which we have tried to run, but, of course, we have made errors and mistakes.

Royal Commission on the Press 1947–49, Question session on 18 March 1948, London: HMSO, Cmd 7416, pp. 154–5.

5.2 Other proprietorial styles: Cecil King at IPC (Daily Mirror group)

The spectre of Beaverbrook at the helm caricatures the nature of control in news organisations and it irons out the great differences that exist. Lord Rothermere, at Associated Newspapers Ltd, apparently worked in a different way and the policy of the papers 'on particular topics was settled by discussion between the editors and himself' (Cmd 7700, June 1949, p. 44).

Cecil King, who was in charge of the Daily Mirror group in the 1950s and 1960s, may not have owned the Mirror group but he was still able to exercise significant degrees of power. He was eventually dismissed as Chairman of IPC when he spearheaded a campaign to oust Harold Wilson, the Labour Prime Minister, in 1968.

... how was policy decreed [in *The Mirror*]? Lord Shawcross, as Chairman of the Royal Commission on the Press in 1961, probed this question with Cecil King and me [Hugh Cudlipp]. A misunderstanding had arisen from a memorandum submitted to the Commission by the Company:

Shawcross: You say there is a committee to discuss strategy?

King: There is no committee; there are only two of us – Cudlipp and myself.

King told the Commission that he met the Editors of the daily and Sunday papers 'very, very occasionally'. He then explained: 'I would say that on editorial policy Hugh Cudlipp and I, who have been directors together for very many years, work closely and are in general agreement on what sort of line we are going to take, I suppose I see him nearly every day, and if anything fresh crops up we decide what we are going to do, but I rarely see the Editors. He sees the Editors and the Editors are responsible to him.' ...

King's Law did not always prevail.... Not always, but occasionally, King respected views sincerely held by others in opposition to his own. A frontal clash of opinion was provoked by the Suez Crisis of 1956. In the initial stage Cecil [King] and I were diametrically opposed to the question of military initiative but the problem was resolved in a civilised manner. [Though King was in favour of British policy] it was decided that the *Mirror* should support international action to keep the Canal free for all navigation and to set up an international agency to run the Canal. The *Mirror* did not support aggression by Britain.

H. Cudlipp, *Walking on the Water*, London: The Bodley Head, 1976, pp. 224, 225–7.

5.3 Other proprietorial styles: Roy Thomson (*Sunday Times*)

A very different character altogether was Lord Roy Thomson, sometime owner of the *Sunday Times*. Thomson's view of himself as proprietor was set out when he gave evidence to the 1961–62 Royal Commission on the Press.

8320. Mr Thomson, you say that you exercise no editorial control. How are the editors appointed to these numerous papers? – I can say this very honestly. I have never in appointing an editor had any consideration to his political views....

I honestly and sincerely believe that the only way that my business can prosper, and that any multiple ownership of newspapers can prosper, is on a basis of complete delegation of editorial authority ...

My purpose is to run newspapers as a business ... To make money. That is what you do business for. I believe newspapers are a free enterprise business. I think there is no future for them unless they are run on that basis.

Evidence to the Royal Commission on the Press 1961–62 (Chairman: Lord Shawcross), *Report*, London: HMSO, Cmnd 1811, September 1962, pp. 622–3.

5.4 Other proprietorial styles: Rupert Murdoch # 1

Rupert Murdoch's style was uncomplicated: he was in charge of the newspapers and he directed them. Those who had encountered Murdoch knew the dangers because they had experienced them. Stafford Somerfield, editor of the *News of the World* from 1960 to 1970, recalls how he found out that Murdoch was able to overcome all regulatory obstacles to purchasing the paper: 'In the City they are saying that a coach and horses has been driven through the Takeover Code' (Somerfield, 1979: 171).

Murdoch was used to telling Editors what to do, and I was used to having my own way. That, in a nutshell, was the difficulty. To the Royal Commission on the Press [1961–62], Carr [then owner of the *News of the World*] had said: 'I cannot remember issuing a directive to the Editor. The policy of this paper is laid down by the board and the Editor interprets it.' I was resolved not to change the situation ...

Murdoch's way was different. 'I did not come all this way not to interfere,' he said. He might have talked about co-operation or working together, but not 'interfering'....

I was ushered in [to my appointment]. 'I want your resignation,' said Murdoch. 'I never resign,' I said.... I walked out of his room. The whole episode had taken three minutes.... The three-minute interview inspired an old friend, another sacked editor, to wire: 'Why did it take three minutes, you talkative bastard?'

S. Somerfield, *Banner Headlines*, Sussex: Scan Books, 1979, pp. 187, 192.

5.5   Other proprietorial styles: Rupert Murdoch # 2

It was a situation that was replayed in the editorial offices of *The Sun*.

If Murdoch was in London he would sometimes join in [editorial] discussions, contributing various wooden-headed editorial suggestions which Lamb [Larry, editor] constantly hoped would be quietly forgotten. The two men clashed often, particularly over the editorial, of which Lamb was so proud. Murdoch would compare the *Sun* and the *Mirror* page by page every day wherever he was in the world. If he was in London the exercise would take place in his ... office. He would lay the papers next to each other and flick through the pages, complaining if he thought the Mirror had done better on any particular story. 'Why did you print this dreadful rubbish?' he would ask Lamb as he leafed through the pages. 'What's all this crap about poofters?' he would enquire when there was a fleeting reference to homosexuality.

P. Chippendale and C. Horrie, *Stick it up Your Punter: The Rise and Fall of the Sun*, London: Heinemann, 1990, p. 45.

5.6   Other proprietorial styles: Rupert Murdoch # 3

Harold Evans, sometime editor of the *Sunday Times*, re-
corded a similar set of circumstances. Murdoch had
succeeded in taking over the whole Times Newspaper group
without the matter being referred to the Monopolies Commission initially on the grounds that 'there is an exemption
under Section 58 for a loss-making company' (Evans, 1984:
159) (see 5.12). One of Evans's major concerns was that of
editorial freedom and he sought to rein in Murdoch's power
and room for manoeuvre. A group of national independent
directors were appointed to act as a buffer between the
proprietor and the editor, and Evans staked much on this
arrangement only to find it a charade.

It was Mrs Thatcher [Prime Minister] who arranged for Rupert
Murdoch's acquisition to escape a reference to the Monopolies Commission.... A newspaper merger unprecedented in newspaper history
went through in three days. In such a rapid process it is perhaps
understandable that he [John Biffen, the Minister] overlooked, or his
official allowed him to overlook, £4.6 million of revenue and
£700,000 of *Sunday Times* profit, so that as regards *The Sunday
Times* he failed to apply the provisions of the Fair Trading Act of
1973....

Evans [to Murdoch]: 'Well, if you get [the newspapers], you're
going to have to satisfy us on independence, on the idea of public
trusteeship ('Sure, sure'.) and no commercial interference. We want
to maintain *The Sunday Times* as a campaigning, investigating
paper.'

He was unfazed ...

He [Murdoch] guaranteed that the editors would have control of
the political policy of their newspapers; that they would have freedom within fixed annual budgets; that the editors would not be subject to instruction from either the proprietor or management on the
selection and balance of news and opinion; that instructions to journalists would be given only by the editor; and that any future sale of
the titles would require the agreement of a majority of the independent national directors. In my year as editor of *The Times*, Murdoch
broke all these guarantees.... he was reminded of the undertakings to
the Secretary of State. 'They're not worth the paper they are written
on' Murdoch replied.

H. Evans, *Good Times, Bad Times*, London: Coronet, 1984, pp. 185, 163, 489–90.

5.7   Other proprietorial styles: Rupert Murdoch # 4

For many, Rupert Murdoch was significantly different from
past proprietors.

It seems Murdoch keeps a healthy eye on the world around him and
lets his editors know his feelings loudly whenever he meets them.
Most of the time he lets them evaluate his feelings themselves. Beyond
that Murdoch fiercely detests 'news management' and it seems unfair
for his critics to infer that his involvements are politically devious....

With the move to London, however, we are dealing with something completely different. The motivation was no longer to produce
bigger, better newspapers. It was self-ambition and challenge. The
fact that his successful bid for the News of the World Organization
was quickly followed by a fabulous Fleet Street success story, is great
in itself. But by then all the original motives must have changed....

... Murdoch will not be satisfied until he has conquered America
and when he has done that he will not be satisfied until he has conquered the world. Whatever the original motives were, they are now
no longer only a matter of having better newspapers, but of having
more newspapers. The fundamental Murdoch dream of a family
dynasty has ceased to be an Australian concept but one of world proportions.

S. Regan, *Rupert Murdoch: A Business Biography*, London: Angus and
Robertson, 1976, pp. 191, 241.

5.8   Other proprietorial styles: the Scott Trust # 1

Not all newspaper groups, however, operate in the same way
and the outstanding example of difference is that of *The
Guardian*, which is, in effect, owned by the Scott Trust.

The Scott Trust was created in 1936 with two main aims in mind.
First, to maintain the journalistic and commercial principles pursued

by C.P. Scott, the Manchester Guardian's editor for 50 years, and also for many years its proprietor. Second, to avoid crippling death duties....

The Trust was intended to be more than a mere device for dealing with death duties. John Scott [C. P. Scott's son] wished to secure the continuity and editorial independence of the Manchester Guardian in the way his father had shaped it. To do so, in a remarkable act of public benefaction, he voluntarily divested himself and his family of holdings worth over £1 million at that time....

The present Scott Trust still operates under the Deed of 1948. It owns The Guardian Media Group plc, a multi-media holding company created in 1993 as a successor to the Guardian and Manchester Evening News plc.... The Group has two divisions. The National Newspaper Division comprises only the *Guardian* and the *Observer*. The Publications and Communications Division, however, includes all of the ... Group's other holdings ... In addition, the Group has substantial investments in broadcasting, including ... GMTV....

The trustee's functions today are these:

A To secure the Trust's own continuity by renewing its membership and by dealing with threats to its existence;

B To monitor the organisation, financial management and overall strategy of the Group, holding the Board accountable for its performance;

C To appoint and 'in extreme circumstances' to dismiss the editors of the *Guardian*, the *Manchester Evening News* and the *Observer*;

D To act as a 'court of appeals' in the event of any dispute between the editorial and managerial sides of the operation.

When a new editor is appointed to the *Guardian* he is enjoined by the chairman of the Trust to carry on the paper along 'the same lines and in the same spirit as heretofore.' ... The 1948 [Trust] Deed put the sentiment differently, stipulating that the papers 'shall be carried on as nearly as may be upon the same principles as they have heretofore been conducted.'...

The Trustees evidently find it hard to conceive of circumstances under which they must be asked to intervene in the *Guardian*'s editorial content. Alastair Hetherington put it thus: 'If the trustees became alarmed at a shift in policy – and it would have to be a pretty drastic one before they became alarmed – they might at least say it would be nice to have a discussion with the editor.' ...

... As the British press becomes concentrated in fewer hands, those who seek to increase – or even now just to maintain – the range of public voices might well consider whether Trust ownership could help them secure their goals.

P. Schlesinger, *The Scott Trust*, London: Scott Trust, 1994, pp. 9, 17, 21, 23, 25.

5.9 Other proprietorial styles: the Scott Trust # 2

In the eyes of the 1974–77 Royal Commission the nature of the Scott Trust was not without its problems, so its adoption would present its own set of difficulties.

4.13 ... Of the publishers of national newspapers, in six cases, ultimate control would appear to rest with an individual or with a family or their trusts, although the responsibility for day to day control is that of the board of directors. Only in the case of Reed International (and later the *Observer* under Atlantic Richfield) are the shares widely held. We have received evidence which suggests that, where newspaper companies are owned by large holding companies, their day to day running, including matters of editorial policy, is almost invariably left entirely to the newspaper subsidiary. Reference to superior companies is generally limited either to matters of strategic policy or approval for capital expenditure programmes. Moreover, the management of the newspaper company is generally separate from that of the other activities of the holding company.

4.14 The Guardian and Manchester Evening News Limited is the only national newspaper publisher owned by a specially constituted trust. They told us in evidence that their trust had been a prime factor in securing the survival, independence and character of their newspapers but that newspapers owned by a non-commercial trust must, as a group, contrive to make profits and could not survive unless they did. While this trust may have secured the survival of *The Guardian*, the typical family trust can be an embarrassment in preserving a loss-making newspaper. In such cases a trust is less flexible than personal ownership because of the fiduciary duty owed by the trustees to the beneficiaries.

Royal Commission on the Press 1974–77 (Chairman: O. R. McGregor), *Final Report*, London: HMSO, Cmnd 6810, July 1977, p. 24.

5.10   Other proprietorial styles: the Scott Trust # 3

The high ideals of the Trust were, for some, only that. That
was the view of Andrew Jaspan, a short-lived editor of *The
Observer* in the 1990s. He was in charge of *The Observer* at a
time when its relationship with *The Guardian* was being reassessed as a consequence of the merger of the two. He none-
theless saw the Trust as an organisation worth working for,
though he was to stay in the post for only a year.

When they told me that they would give me the necessary support and
time to restore the fortunes of the *Observer*, I believed them. Other
newspaper owners, I reasoned, might be expected to break such
assurances, but not the Scott Trust, which had loyally supported Peter Preston, the editor of the *Guardian*, for 20 years.

True, there was the awkward question of my predecessor's fate....
[He] had been removed after little more than a year. I was told that,
unlike myself, he lacked Sunday newspaper experience. Furthermore,
the Scott Trust censured itself for rushing into his appointment and
resolved that in future the appointments procedure would conform
with the *Guardian*'s more laborious but consultative 'good employer'
practice....

Peter Preston was away ... and some members of the Scott Trust
met and agreed to topple Preston as editor-in-chief of the *Guardian*
and *Observer* and put Rusbridger's [editor of *The Guardian*] take-
over plans for the *Observer* into operation.

Rusbridger duly became executive editor of the *Observer*.... The
Trust (dispensing with its appointments procedure) also agreed to
appoint Will Hutton as editor, even though they had rejected him a
year earlier....

So that's how my dream of helping restore the fortunes of the
Observer ended.... The Guardian and the Scott Trust have to all
intents and purposes killed off the separate and distinct character of
the *Observer*. The *Observer* is now simply an adjunct of the *Guardian* (G3 the wits call it, in the pecking order after the *Guardian*'s tab-
loid section, which Rusbridger created)....

So where did I go wrong? Perhaps Ben Bradlee, the distinguished
former editor of *The Washington Post*, knows the answer.... 'First,
pick the right owner.' (I thought I had.) Then, for a newspaper to
work, its owners must understand 'that choosing an editor is a waste

of time unless it is followed by a pledge of total support'.

Without that total support I lasted barely a year. Bradlee would doubtless say, that proves my point, boy.

A. Jaspan, 'The Trust that went bust', *New Statesman*, 12 July 1996, pp. 16–19.

CROSS-MEDIA OWNERSHIP

> Concerns about ownership and the undue influence that ownership can bring with it, particularly if it extends across several newspapers or across newspapers and periodicals, was something which Commissions regularly addressed. With the growth of commercial television, the concern became one of ownership across different media.

5.11 Multiple ownership and diversification of interests, 1960

(36) Proprietors who publish a number of newspapers and periodicals may benefit from economies, but manpower economies are less than might be supposed. Multiple undertakings can also provide common services which would be beyond the reach of individual newspapers in their groups.

(37) Some aspects of multiple ownership may give a weak publication a better chance of survival; on the other hand multiple ownership may be disadvantageous to a publication. A certain amount of multiple ownership contributes to the maintenance of the number and variety of publications.

(38) Newspapers under common ownership do not necessarily have a common approach to public questions and editors have a reasonable degree of independence.

(39) A number of newspaper undertakings own interests in television. In view of the statutory monopoly enjoyed by television contracting companies, we consider it to be contrary to the public interest for such companies to be controlled by newspaper undertakings. *We recommend* that such arrangements be terminated at the earliest possible date.

(40) The only substantial benefit which newspaper undertakings

usually derive from minority interests in television or from interests in paper-making and other enterprises is the investment income.

Royal Commission on the Press 1961–62 (Chairman: Lord Shawcross), *Report*, London: HMSO, Cmnd 1811, September 1962, Summary of Conclusions and Recommendations.

5.12 Cross-ownership of media, 1977

> The 1974–77 Royal Commission made reference to two aspects of this issue. First, there was the question of newspaper mergers themselves (though it pointed out that most cases were not referred to the Monopolies Commission, para. 14.17); second, there was the issue of national newspapers having interests in commercial television. There were different provisions for ownership of newspapers and radio stations.

14.15 Following the Report of the 1961–62 Royal Commission, the monopolies and mergers legislation was strengthened in 1965 by provisions now contained in the Fair Trading Act 1973. Transfers of controlling interests in daily, Sunday or local newspapers (or newspaper assets) to persons with newspaper interests require the consent of the Secretary of State for Prices and Consumer Protection if such persons already control (or as a result of the transfer would obtain control over) daily, Sunday or local newspapers having an average daily circulation ... of 500,000 copies or more. A controlling interest is defined as a holding of 25% or more. The Secretary of State is required to refer all such proposed transfers to the ... Commission within one month of application; but if he is satisfied that the newspaper concerned is not economic as a separate newspaper, he *may* give his consent without reference to the Commission if the paper is to continue as a separate newspaper and the case is one of urgency, and *shall* do so if he is satisfied that it is not intended to continue the paper as a separate newspaper. He *may* also consent without reference to the Commission if the paper has an average daily circulation of not more than 25,000 copies. The circulation figures of 500,000 and 25,000 may be varied by statutory instrument.
14.16 On a reference, the Commission are required to report

whether the transfer may be expected to operate against the public interest, taking into account all relevant matters and in particular 'the need for accurate presentation of news and free expression of opinion'....

15.6 ... the IBA have confirmed to us as their policy ... that the Authority are not opposed to the ownership of shares in programme companies by newspapers, and in fact regard it as valuable. But they are opposed to the control of any programme company by a single newspaper or press interest....

Royal Commission on the Press 1974–77 (Chairman: O. R. McGregor), *Final Report*, London: HMSO, Cmnd 6810, July 1977, pp. 131, 142–3.

5.13 The relaxation of the rules governing media ownership in the 1990s

In December 1993, Parliament's decision to 'relax the rules governing ownership of regional Channel 3 licences ended the former prohibition of common control of any two of the largest nine licensees' (Cm 2872, 1995, p. 8). By 1997, there were three major groups in charge of national commercial television, i.e. Channel 3. The three were Carlton Television (which also owns Central and Westcountry), United Newspapers and Media (which also owns Meridian and Anglia) and Granada (which also owns London Weekend Television and Yorkshire Tyne-Tees).

All these changes were within the framework set out by the Department of National Heritage's vision of the future of commercial television (and of the BBC). But the liberalisation of rules was also to permit for a greater element of cross-ownership as between newspapers, television and radio. Although the proposals did make note of the need to promote diversity in media material, they did not really address the contradiction that diversity might be put at risk through the creation of stronger competitive media groups or the operation of the free market.

2. ... the Government believes that a number of changes should now be made in order to preserve the diversity of the broadcast and press media in the UK, whilst introducing greater flexibility in ownership

to reflect the needs and aspirations of the industry, against a background of accelerating technological change, including the introduction of digital broadcasting....

The government believes that the long term regulatory regime must:

– continue to safeguard the public interest in a free and diverse media;

– allow the media industry to evolve in a way that exploits the opportunities created by technological change; and

– be clear and easily understood....

5.20 It is against [a background of technological convergence] that the traditional relationship between the press and broadcasting sectors needs to be reassessed. The changes facing the media industry challenge the existing approach to ownership regulation. Alliances between television and newspaper companies are a logical and natural product of the economic and technological dynamics of the industry and will allow a healthy interchange of skills and creativity for the benefit of the consumer....

6.24 The Government wishes to create a regulatory framework that permits some newspaper groups to expand into television, and vice versa, but which also maintains a pluralistic and diverse media industry. It therefore proposes to establish a circulation threshold, below which newspaper groups will be free to own outright television broadcasters, and vice versa. Subject to the public interest considerations [regarding the promotion of diversity] the Government proposes to set a threshold at 20 per cent of national newspaper circulation market share. Companies below that level will be able to apply to control up to 15 per cent of the total television market (by audience share) including the control of up to:

– two regional Channel 3 licences ... ; or

– one regional Channel 3 licence and the Channel 5 licence; or

– one regional Channel 3 licence and the Channel 3 licence.

Newspapers and radio

6.28 The arrangements set out ... for newspapers and television will be replicated for radio.... Only one national radio licence could be controlled, and approvals for local radio licences would not be given for newspapers with more than 30% of the circulation in the particular locality....

Television

6.29 ... the Government will also simplify the rules concerning the control of television licences by:

(i) maintaining the current two-licence limit on regional Channel 3 licences; but enabling broadcasters to expand to up to 15% of total television audience share thereafter, including the control of up to:

– two regional Channel 3 licences (but not both London licences); or

– one regional Channel 3 and the Channel 5 licence; or

– one regional Channel 3 licence and the national Channel 3 licence;

(ii) abolishing the rules which limit ownership between the various means of delivery (terrestrial, cable and satellite) ...

6.30 ... terrestrial broadcasters will be allowed to have controlling interests in satellite and cable companies, provided their total interests do not exceed 15% of total television audience share (measured with the inclusion of public service broadcasters). Satellite and cable companies will be able to have outright ownership of Channel 3 or Channel 5 licences subject to the 15% total television market and the two-licence limits ...

6.31 The current rules for ownership of non-domestic satellite broadcasters and cable operators have already allowed for a much higher level of investment by newspapers in those sectors than in terrestrial television. The Government has therefore decided that it would be appropriate to exclude those satellite and cable companies with more than 20% ownership by newspaper groups above the circulation threshold ... from the new television freedoms in 6.29. If a satellite or cable company has more than 20% ownership by any newspaper group or groups with a national circulation share of more than 20%, it will therefore continue to be restricted to a 20% holding in one Channel 3 or the Channel 5 licence, and 5% in any further such licences.

Department of National Heritage, *Media Ownership: The Government's Proposals*, London: HMSO, Cm 2872, 1995, pp. 1, 19, 26–7.

THE PRESS AND PRIVACY

At regular intervals, there are calls for a tightening of the rules governing press behaviour. But the need to protect privacy sits uneasily against a system where newspapers regulate themselves and where there is no legal framework to prevent excesses. One of a legion of cases which brought the press into 'disrepute' concerned the actor Gordon Kaye. Kaye had been seriously injured in the hurricane of 1987. Whilst lying in hospital, he was photographed by two *Sunday Sport* journalists. Although Kaye's agent sought an injunction to stop the publication of the photographs, the judges considering the appeal 'recognize[d] their near total impotence. "It is well-known that in English law there is no right of privacy, and accordingly there is no right of action for breach of a person's privacy," said Lord Justice Glidewell' (Snoddy, 1993: 94).

5.14   The 1947–49 Royal Commission and plans for a Press Council

Historically, there has been a predilection for self-regulation rather than a statutory framework to deal with such abuses of newspaper power. The problem arose when the media (mainly newspapers) defined the 'public interest' as 'whatever interested the public'. The 1947–49 Royal Commission was against any means of control being imposed on the press, though it did make a case for a body to regulate and develop the newspaper industry.

683. ... We prefer to seek the means of maintaining the free expression of opinion and the greatest practicable accuracy in the presentation of news, and, generally, a proper relationship between the Press and society, primarily in the Press itself.

684. Accordingly *we recommend:–*

1. That the Press should establish a General Council of the Press consisting of 25 members representing proprietors, editors, and other journalists, and having lay members amounting to about 20 per cent of the total, including the chairman....

The objects of the General Council should be to safeguard the freedom of the Press; to encourage the growth of the sense of responsibil-

ity and public service amongst all engaged in the profession of journalism – that is, in the editorial production of newspapers ... and to
further the efficiency of the profession and the well-being of those
who practise it.

In furtherance [it] should take such action as it thinks fit:

(1) to keep under review any developments likely to restrict the
supply of information of public interest and importance;

(2) to improve the methods of recruitment, education, and training
for the profession; ...

(4) by censuring undesirable types of journalistic conduct, and by
all other means to build up a code in accordance with the highest
professional standards.... it should have the right to consider ... complaints, to deal with these complaints in whatever manner may seem
to it practicable and appropriate, and to include in its annual report
any action under this heading; ...

(8) to study developments in the Press which may tend towards
greater concentration and monopoly; ...

Royal Commission on the Press 1947–49 (Chairman: Sir W. D. Ross),
Report, London: HMSO, Cmd 7700, June 1949, pp. 177–8.

5.15   The 1961–62 Royal Commission
and the Press Council

The 1961–62 Royal Commission made its own recommendations on this matter.

Summary of Conclusions and Recommendations
The General Council of the Press

(51) *We recommend* that the constituent bodies should reconstitute
the General Council of the Press so as to comply with the recommendation of the 1949 Commission that there should be a lay chairman
and a substantial lay membership.

(52) *We recommend* that the Government should specify a time
limit after which legislation would be introduced for the establishment of such a Press Council, if in the meantime it had not been set up
voluntarily.

(53) *We recommend* that the Council should be provided by its
constituent bodies with sufficient financial and other resources to

enable it not only to effectively carry out its present functions but also to

(i) report publicly in changes in the ownership, control and growth of Press undertakings;

(ii) publish up-to-date statistical information relevant to concentration of ownership;

(iii) [ensure] that newspapers should bear the name of the company or individual in ultimate control of their affairs;

(iv) act as a tribunal to hear complaints from editors and journalists of undue influence by advertisers ... [or] their superiors to distort the truth or otherwise engage in unprofessional conduct.

Royal Commission on the Press 1961–62 (Chairman: Lord Shawcross), *Report*, London: HMSO, Cmnd 1811, September 1962, p. 117.

5.16   The 1974–77 Royal Commission and the Press Council

Had things changed significantly by the time of the third Royal Commission?

20.4 ... The General Council of the Press was a central recommendation in the [1947–49 Royal Commission Report] but was not implemented until 1953 after the threat of legislation. The Council was then made up of 25 representatives drawn only from the profession, and did not contain independent or lay members, as the ... Commission had recommended.

20.5 The second ... Commission recommended the appointment not only of lay members but also of a lay chairman. As a result, the Press Council (its name was changed at the time) was reconstituted under an independent chairman with five lay members out of 25.

20.6 The constitution of the Press Council was changed again in 1973, following the Report of the Committee on Privacy.... Lay members were increased to ten out of 30. The constitution of the complaints committee was changed to give six lay members and six press members under the chairmanship of the Chairman of the Press Council....

20.10 ... In response to ... criticisms and suggestions, the Press Council re-drafted its articles of constitution ...

(a) To preserve the established freedom of the British press.

(b) To maintain the character of the ... press in accordance with the highest professional and commercial standards.

(c) To consider complaints about the conduct of the press ... to deal with these ...

(d) To keep under review developments likely to restrict the supply of information of public interest and importance.

(e) To report publicly on developments that may tend towards greater concentration and monopoly ... and to publish statistical information relating thereto.

(f) To make representations on appropriate occasions to the Government ...

(g) To publish periodical reports ...

20.15 ... We do not believe that the Press Council can expect ready acceptance of the arguments both that it is independent of press interests and that it is a self-regulating body which must therefore maintain a majority of press representatives....

Chapter 23: Summary of Recommendations
[We recommend that the Council should be] constituted of an equal number of lay and press representatives under an independent chairman....

That the Press Council extend its doctrine of the right of reply and uphold a newspaper's making available space to those it has criticised inaccurately.

That the Press Council should change its position on the two important questions of accuracy and bias, so that inaccuracy even if subsequently corrected, should be *prima facie* evidence for upholding a complaint, and that contentious opinions based on inaccurate information should be grounds for censure.

Royal Commission on the Press 1974–77 (Chairman: O. R. McGregor), *Final Report*, London: HMSO, Cmnd 6810, July 1977, pp. 235–6.

5.17 The failure of self-regulation

The concern with privacy, and the Press Council's failure to deal with the issue adequately, was not new. Although the Press Council had argued that 'there has been a great improvement in the behaviour of newspapers in the last twenty years' (Cmnd 6810, July 1977, p. 210, para. 20.60), there were those who thought differently.

20.61 The Press Council and those who generally support it hold that publicity and condemnation are the most effective sanctions which can be used against journalists. Those in the profession have suggested to us that they really do feel the Press Council breathing down their necks as they practise, and plead that any stronger sanctions would be impracticable and undesirable....

20.62 On the other hand, the critics ... think that sanction of publicised criticism is inadequate. They argue that only fines or suspension would make a real difference to the conduct of journalists....

20.64 In our opinion, there are still flagrant breaches of acceptable standards.... A letter in *The Times* [22 November 1975] protested about intrusions into privacy in a case in which two girls had drowned during a school swimming lesson:

The following day, on their return from the Coroner's office, one of the fathers could not park his car anywhere near to his home as the whole road was crammed with television and radio recording cars and cars of newspaper reporters. To reach the privacy of his home the father had to run the gauntlet of 'Who do you think is to blame? Are you going to press charges? Oh come on, help us a bit. I've got a job to do', etc. The reports have been pregnant with innuendoes and a desire to spark off a confrontation.

Clearly there was no acceptance there of high standards of journalistic behaviour, notwithstanding the risk of an adverse adjudication by the Press Council.

Royal Commission on the Press 1974–77 (Chairman: O. R. McGregor), *Final Report*, London: HMSO, Cmnd 6810, July 1977, pp. 210–11.

5.18   The continued failure of self-regulation

The Gordon Kaye case (see 5.14) and other cases in the 1990s kept the issue of privacy and legislation on the boil. Other cases followed, including one involving David Mellor, the National Heritage Secretary. Mellor was to declare that with regard to matters of privacy and intrusion, the press was on parole. It was 'drinking at the last chance saloon'.

In view of the mounting concern, the Press Council issued an updated code of practice in 1991. One aim, clearly, was to stem criticism by showing that action was being taken to limit excesses. At issue, though, was the fact that journalists and editors were only too ready to bend the code to get a scoop.

Accuracy: It is the duty of newspapers not to publish deliberately or carelessly inaccuracies or statements designed to mislead, and to correct promptly and with due prominence significant inaccuracies which they have published, or misleading statements, for which they are responsible, apologising for these where appropriate.

Opportunity to reply: It is the duty of newspapers to allow a fair opportunity for reply when reasonably called for.

Privacy: Publishing material or making inquiries about the private lives of individuals without their consent is not acceptable unless these are in the public interest overriding the right of privacy. The Press Council's Declaration of Principle on Privacy should be observed.

Comment and fact: Newspapers are free to be partisan but they should distinguish between comment and fact. Conjecture should not be elevated into statements of fact.

Subterfuge: Newspapers and journalists serving them should use straightforward means to obtain information or pictures. Their use of subterfuge can be justified only to obtain material which ought to be published in the public interest and which could not be obtained by other means.

Payments for articles: Payments or offers of payment for stories, pictures, or information should not be made to witnesses or potential witnesses in current criminal proceedings or to people engaged in crime or their associates except where the material concerned ought to be published in the public interest, and the payment is necessary to enable this. The Press Council's Declaration of Principle on Payment for Articles should be observed.

Intrusion into grief: Newspapers and journalists serving them should in general avoid intruding into personal grief. Inquiries should be carried out with sympathy and discretion.

Innocent relatives: Newspapers should exercise care and discretion before identifying relatives of persons convicted or accused of crime where the reference to them is not directly relevant to the matter reported.

Interviewing children: Journalists should not normally interview a child under the age of 16 in the absence of, or without the consent of, a parent or other adult responsible for the child.

Children in sex cases: Save in exceptional circumstances newspapers should not, even where the law permits it, identify children under the age of 16 as victims, witnesses, or defendants involved in cases concerning sexual offences.

Rape victims: Newspapers should not identify victims of rape, or publish material likely to contribute to such identification.

Pictures: Newspapers should refrain from publishing pictures which needlessly exacerbate grief or cause distress.

Race and colour: Newspapers should not publish material likely to encourage discrimination on grounds of race or colour and newspapers should avoid reference to people's race or colour in prejudicial or pejorative contexts unless they are directly relevant to the story.

Financial journalism: Journalists should not use for their own profit financial information they receive in advance of its general publication. The Press Council's Declaration of Principle on Financial Journalism should be observed.

Hospitals: Journalists making inquiries at hospitals or similar institutions should identify themselves to a responsible official before entering, except in very rare cases where information which ought to be disclosed could not otherwise be obtained.

Confidential sources: Journalists have an obligation to protect confidential sources of information.

'Press Council's 16-point code of practice', *The Guardian*, 16 March 1992, p. 2.

5.19   The Calcutt inquiry

The Inquiry into Privacy and Related Matters (Cm 1102, 1990) was chaired by David Calcutt. Almost three years later, he was asked to conduct a review of press self-regulation. Around the time of the first inquiry, two private members' bills had been put before Parliament and these dealt with matters of press intrusion into private lives. In his review, Calcutt first provided a Résumé of the Privacy Committee's

Report. This was followed by a summary of differences between the Committee's recommendations and those of the industry.

2 Résumé of the Privacy Committee's Report ...

2.5 The Report [on Privacy] ... was unanimous. It recognised the balance to be struck between freedom of expression and an individual's right to privacy. The Committee acknowledged that freedom of expression was fundamental in a democratic society, but conceded that this could not be at the expense of other important rights, including an individual's right to privacy.

2.6 The Committee made a number of recommendations.... That package can be summarised in the following way:

(i) any new means of redress needed to be carefully targeted, and should not range more widely than was necessary to meet existing gaps in protection;

(ii) ... the introduction of any new wide-ranging statutory civil right of 'infringement of privacy' ... would not then be appropriate;

(iii) The most blatant forms of intrusion – practices involving door-stepping, bugging, and the use of long-range cameras – should be outlawed;

(iv) the existing statutory restrictions on reporting should be strengthened so as to provide added protection for children and the victims of sexual offences;

(v) the press' own arrangements for voluntary self-regulation should be revised, and strengthened as greatly as possible by the introduction of a new Press Complaints Commission; and

(vi) if the press failed to demonstrate that non-statutory self-regulation could be made to work effectively, a statutory press tribunal for handling complaints should be introduced....

3.94 Overall, there are significant differences between the Press Complaints Commission which the Privacy Committee recommended and the Press Complaints Commission which has been set up by the industry. The principal differences are these:

(i) The members ... are appointed ... by a body which is the creature of the industry.

(ii) There are signs that the Commission is once again asserting, as the Press Council did, a positive role for the Commission in defending press freedom.

185

(iii) The Commission operates a code of practice produced and monitored, not by the Commission, but by the press industry.

(iv) The ... code of practice reduces ... the protection ... proposed for individuals, and it does not hold the balance fairly.

(v) ... the code of practice widens considerations of 'public interest', and thereby significantly reduces an individual's protection.

(vi) The Commission is generally unwilling to operate a hot line.

(vii) The Commission is presently unwilling to initiate inquiries.

Appendix C

The Privacy Committee's proposed Code of Practice ...	Press Industry's Code of Practice
4 Privacy	4 Privacy
(i) Making enquiries about the personal lives of individuals without their consent is not generally acceptable.	Intrusions and enquiries into an individual's private life without his or her consent are not generally acceptable and publication can only be justified when in the public interest. This would include:
(ii) Publishing material about the personal [lives] of individuals without their consent is not generally acceptable.	(i) Detecting or exposing crime or serious misdemeanour.
(iii) An intrusion into an individual's personal life can be justified only for the purpose of detecting or exposing crime or seriously anti-social conduct, protecting public health or safety, or preventing the public being misled by some public statement or action of that individual.	(ii) Detecting or exposing seriously anti-social conduct. (iii) Protecting public health and safety. (iv) Preventing the public from being misled by some statement or action of that individual.
(iv) An individual's personal life includes matters of health, home, personal relationships, correspondence and documents but does not include his trade or business.	
7 Harassment	Harassment
(i) Journalists should neither obtain nor seek to obtain	(i) Journalists should neither obtain information nor pictures

information or pictures through intimidation, harassment or trespass.

(ii) They should not persist in telephoning or questioning individuals after having been asked to desist and should not remain on their property after having been asked to leave....

(iv) They should not photograph individuals on private property without their consent unless it is necessary (for the purpose of detecting or exposing crime or seriously anti-social conduct, protecting public health or safety, or preventing the public from being misled by some public statement or action of an individual).

through intimidation or harassment.

(ii) Unless their inquiries are in the public interest, journalists should not photograph individuals on private property without their consent; should not persist in telephoning or questioning individuals after having been asked to desist and should not remain on their property after having been asked to leave and should not follow them.

The public interest would include:

(a) Detecting or exposing crime or serious misdemeanour.

(b) Detecting or exposing anti-social conduct.

(c) Protecting public health and safety.

(d) Preventing the public from being misled by some public statement or action of that individual or organisation.

Review of Press Self-Regulation (Chairman: Sir D. Calcutt QC), Department of National Heritage, London: HMSO, Cm 2135, 1993, pp. 4–5, 24, 80–2.

5.20   The 'last chance saloon': near the end of the road?

David Calcutt's review of the system of self-regulation was anything but complementary.

5.29 In my view the press has demonstrated that it is itself unwilling to put in place a regulatory system which commands the confidence, not only of the press (which I am sure it does) but also of the public, and which fairly holds the balance between them; and I see no realistic possibility of that being changed by voluntary action.

5.30 Too many fundamental changes to the present arrangements would be needed; ...

5.31 Nothing that I have learnt about the Press has led me to conclude that the press would now be willing to make, or that it would in fact make, the changes which would be needed. Indeed, the way in which the Commission has been set up ... leads me to the conclusion that it would not be willing to make and would not make those changes....

Review of Press Self-Regulation (Chairman: Sir D. Calcutt QC), Department of National Heritage, London: HMSO, Cm 2135, 1993, pp. 42–3.

5.21 The editors respond to the demands for legislation on privacy

Though the various reports concerning the work of the press and its general behaviour were very critical and made demands for some action, newspaper editors quickly mounted a rearguard action to prevent any such possibility. In February 1994 the Association of British Editors produced a booklet which critically examined the work of Calcutt and made a strong plea that the press be left alone.

That plea was built around an argument that much was already in place which affected the media's behaviour, that legislation would be difficult to draw up, and that ultimately the existing mechanisms – including the appointment of a Privacy Commissioner and newspaper 'ombudsmen' – were sufficiently adequate.

3.1 Few not directly involved have any idea of the scope of the statutory restrictions already operating to prevent media obtaining information or publishing it.... The White Paper *Open Government* (Cm 2290, Annexe B) identified no fewer than 251 existing statutory instruments making it an offence to disclose information. They range from the Abortion Act 1967 ... to the Wireless Telegraphy Act 1949 and the Uncertified Securities Regulations 1992.

3.2 All of these statutory restrictions on the disclosure of information – some justifiable, most not – reduce the media's ability to monitor the performance of government in the public interest. In addition the media operate in the context of a whole range of legislation which contains statutory restrictions or prohibitions on reporting.... They range from the well-known Official Secrets Acts 1911 to 1989 ... to the less discussed sections of the Theft Act 1968 and the Unsolicited Goods and Services Act 1971.

3.3 In addition to legal restrictions on the media, there are a number of bodies already charged with media regulation in one way or another....

3.6 It is clear from the above that historically, via statute and the development of common law, Parliament and the courts have progressively provided increased protection to the privacy of the individual over the years....

3.17 The head of steam behind the proposed [legislation] is not fired by any substantial concern about the wider legal picture of privacy. There is equally no evidence of public concern about privacy and the broadcasting media. There is clearly political concern about actual or alleged invasion of privacy by the Press. Even on this narrow front, though there may be a problem, no evidence has been presented of extensive invasion of privacy by magazines or regional and local papers. Unless this conclusion is contradicted by evidence, the arguments presented to date are an inadequate and unsatisfactory basis for the introduction of an entire new civil wrong of infringement of privacy, with potential and undesired consequences over such a substantial range of law unconnected with the Press....

5.16 In summary, we find no convincing evidence that a statutory replacement for the existing Press Complaints Commission would on balance serve better to protect the legitimate privacy of the private citizen. On the contrary we see substantial legal and practical disadvantages in such a proposal....

6.6 *Our conclusion is that a privacy law or any further statutory regulation of the media along the lines proposed would be seriously detrimental to freedom of the press and the freedom to publish, without which a democratic society cannot operate properly.*

Association of British Editors, *Media Freedom and Media Regulation: An Alternative White Paper*, London: ABE, 1994, pp. 8–9, 12, 23, 25.

5.22   Calcutt, Princess Diana, and after:
the new (1997) code of practice

The death of Princess Diana, and the role of the *paparazzi* in that tragedy, fuelled interest in matters of privacy. A new Code of Practice was produced in 1997 and there was renewed hope that the system of self-regulation would, once more, negate the need for legislation. However, a number of stories in 1998 – a minister's son on a drugs charge, a minister's divorce – showed that the press was straining at the leash and that the new Code was going to be severely tested on a regular basis.

Clause 3: Privacy

(i) Everyone is entitled to respect for his or her private and family life, home, health and correspondence. A publication will be expected to justify intrusions into any individual's private life without consent.

(ii) The use of longlens photography to take pictures of people in private places without their consent is unacceptable.

Note: Private places are public or private where there is a reasonable expectation of privacy.

Clause 4: Harassment

(i) Journalists and photographers must neither obtain nor seek to obtain information or pictures through intimidation, harassment or persistent pursuit.

(ii) They must not photograph individuals in private places without their consent; must not persist in telephoning, questioning, pursuing or photographing individuals after having been asked to desist; must not remain on their property after having been asked to leave and must not follow them.

(iii) Editors must ensure that those working for them comply with these requirements and must not publish material from other sources which does not meet these requirements.

C. Dyer, 'Privacy. The media take a shot in the dark', *The Guardian*, 19 December 1997, p. 15.

THE LOBBY AND LOBBY PRACTICES

Another aspect of the media which caused consternation to journalists as well as outsiders was the work routines of Lobby or political correspondents. This was another area of political life which, many felt, was too secretive and which should also be opened up. The history of the Lobby since 1945 highlights both the changing nature of journalism itself and the greater need for openness in the modern era.

5.23 The Lobby rules

The organisation of political journalism has consistently interested students of the mass media: with hints of secret cabals and questionable practices, of outdated arrangements and subservience to politicians, it became an easy target for criticism from those who sought to open up the whole process by which Westminster was reported. The publication of the 1956 Lobby rules in 1970 seemed to confirm suspicions.

Lobby practice
The technique of Lobby journalism can be fully acquired only by experience. It is a technique which brings the journalist into close daily touch with Ministers and Members of Parliament ... and imposes on him a very high standard of responsibility and discretion in making use of the special facilities given him for writing about political affairs....

Individual lobbying
Over a period of seventy-five years the Lobby has been under an obligation not to name informants. Moreover, experience has shown that Ministers and M.P.s talk more freely under the rule of anonymity. In any case, members of the Lobby should always take personal responsibility for their stories and their facts.

It is the Lobby correspondent's primary duty to protect his informants, ...

... do not use information, even if given unconditionally, if you have reason to believe that its publication may constitute a breach of Parliamentary privilege.

Collective lobbying

It has become common practice for Ministers and others to meet the Lobby collectively to give information and answer questions.

Members of the Lobby are under an obligation to keep secret the fact that such meetings are held, and to avoid revealing the sources of their information....

Do not talk about Lobby meetings BEFORE or AFTER they are held, especially in the presence of those not entitled to attend them....

General hints

Do not 'see' anything in the members' Lobby, or in any one of the private rooms or corridors of the Palace of Westminster. You are a guest of Parliament, and it has always been the rule that incidents, pleasant or otherwise, should be treated as private if they happen in those parts of the building to which Lobby correspondents have access ...

Do not run after a Minister or Private member. It is nearly always possible to place oneself in a position to avoid this.

Do not crowd together in the Lobby so as to be conspicuous....

Do not use a notebook, or, as a rule, make notes when in private conversation, in the members' Lobby.

NEVER, in ANY circumstances, make use of anything accidentally overheard in any part of the Palace of Westminster.

J. Tunstall, *The Westminster Lobby Correspondents*, London: Routledge and Kegan Paul, 1970, pp. 124–7.

5.24 The Lobby: attempts at reform

The Lobby system came under sustained attack in the mid-1980s. There were many reasons for this, including consistent leaking, alleged misuse of the Lobby by politicians, Bernard Ingham's stewardship as Margaret Thatcher's press secretary, and general unhappiness over the non-attribution rule (see Harris, 1991). When two newspapers withdrew from the Lobby, an inquiry was instituted. The ensuing report on the Lobby re-affirmed its practices.

In a ballot on October 29 [1986] the Lobby voted by 67 to 55 against a change in the rules of non-attribution in Lobby briefings and by 68 to 58 in favour of an inquiry into Lobby practice. The ballot was held following a special meeting of the Lobby on October 22 called to discuss the *Guardian's* decision to break the rules of non-attribution at Lobby briefings. This followed an instruction by the editor to his political staff to attend the regular meetings of the Prime Minister's press secretary and report what he said and attribute relevant quotations. This in turn followed the *Independent's* decision not to attend Lobby briefings....

The debate [on the Lobby] needs to be seen in the context of changes in the position of the Lobby and in the day-to-day application of the Lobby Practice or rules. The picture of a relatively small number of senior, highly experienced correspondents operating in a very close relationship with Downing Street spokesmen, is long gone.

The Lobby is now larger, less experienced and more fluid in its membership than in the past....

The inquiry has revealed a wide divergence of views, though the evidence received from those with the deepest knowledge of the Lobby system, both as press secretaries and journalists, generally backs the view that the unattributable system has shown itself over the years as the most workable way of getting more information from the Government to the public. However, even some supporters of the present system argue that more on-the-record information should be made available where possible....

... those journalists accredited to be Lobby correspondents who do choose to attend unattributable briefings have an obligation to accept and abide by whatever rules are mutually agreed at the time, as is true with all journalists' relationships with their sources....

The Lobby – and the system of unattributable briefings – represents a far from unique journalistic trade-off between the desire for as much information as possible and as great a degree of attribution as possible. The system of unattributable briefings can be seen ... as 'to seek to influence opinion without accepting responsibility'. How the information is used depends on the talents and judgements of individual journalists, as it always has. As Tom McCaffrey [press secretary to Jim Callaghan, Labour Prime Minister in the late 1970s] put it: 'The Lobby system is a convenience, not a conspiracy.'

The rules of Lobby practice should be simplified, clarified, re-issued and made public.

Anyone who wishes to attend Lobby briefings should give a written undertaking that they are prepared to obey the rules of those meetings....

The Lobby should re-affirm its long-standing commitment to pressing for on-the-record information wherever and whenever practicable – but not where it inhibits the flow of information from the Government to the public....

'To name or not to name? Extracts from official report on parliamentary Lobby practice', *The Guardian*, 9 December 1986.

5.25 Why *The Guardian* returned to the Lobby in 1989

The changes that had taken place – perhaps less real than was trumpeted – were enough to let *The Guardian*, *The Scotsman* and *The Independent* return to the Lobby without losing face.

AFTER almost four years, the *Guardian*'s political team will, from next week, regularly attend the daily briefings given by the Prime Minister's office....

Peter Preston, editor of the *Guardian*, said: 'When, alone, we first withdrew from the system, the central issue was one of attribution. We could not identify clearly for readers the source of the information transmitted by the then Downing Street press secretary.

'We thoroughly disliked a system where – without attribution – the spokesman could indulge in personal denigration as well as contentious background briefing without being identified.

'That situation has changed considerably over the past year. The use of clear formulas for attribution – like "the Prime Minister's Office said . . ." – are accepted. Readers know who is saying what.

'In these circumstances it seems sensible to rejoin the system. We look forward to open and on-the-record briefings in the future. But there has been real progress over the past year and it seems practical to acknowledge that fact.'

'Downing Street source to add flavour', *The Guardian*, 12 October 1991, p. 6.

5.26 New Labour, new (Lobby) rules

The disquiet over Lobby practices and of the practice of non-attribution in particular rumbled on into the 1990s with increasing amounts of information about the sources of briefings becoming available. 'Sources close to the Minister' segued into 'Downing Street sources' and as the doings of press secretaries became more public, the system of non-attribution was strained. In addition, as interest in governmental public relations activity, 'spinning' and 'spin-doctoring' galvanised journalists (if not the public), greater transparency was called for.

The new Labour government of Tony Blair published its plans for reforming the government information service (GIS) in November 1997. Within that reform, there were proposals to change certain Lobby practices, although the press continued to use references to unnamed sources as a means of highlighting political dissent.

2. Any Government needs modern and effective relations with the media. The effective communication and explanation of policy and decisions should not be an after-thought, but an integral part of a democratic Government's duty to govern with consent. The Government has a duty to explain its policies and to do so professionally. The media world is changing fast, with the information age widening the range of news outlets, operating round the clock with increasing immediacy. That changes the way that politics, and the issues of Government, are covered by the media. It places new and exacting demands on the professionals required to communicate the Government's policies to the media and through them the public which elected them.... In this Report we outline changes in a number of areas so this can be achieved, against the background of retaining a politically impartial service and sustaining the trusted values of the GIS embodied in its rules of guidance....

25. *Conventions of Attribution* The Chief Press Secretary's twice-daily briefings of the Lobby are conducted on the assumption that they are off-the-record. The pros and cons of non-attribution have been the subject of continuing debate.

26. We do not intend to rehearse that debate in this report save to note that it is anonymous sources which increasingly dominate political journalism, both news and commentary. A Lobby system which

relies on non-attribution tends to give an unwarranted credibility to those unnamed sources who are always 'senior' and invariably 'close' to whichever Minister is the prime subject of the story.

27. In these circumstances, it becomes ever more important to ensure that authentic Government statements, especially from the Centre, carry due authority. We think there is now a strong case for conducting the twice-daily Lobby briefings on the assumption that they are on-the-record, with the Chief Press Secretary identified as 'the Prime Minister's official spokesman'. We think that the current bar on journalists saying that a briefing has been held, or where, should be removed. We have considered whether the Chief Press Secretary should be named; but we think this could tend to build up an official, appointed to represent the position of his elected masters, too much into a figure in his own right. For the same reason, we think the Lobby's on-the-record briefings should be off-camera and that Ministers should continue to be the public face of Government....

Cabinet Office, *Report on the Working Group on the Government Information Service*, London: Office of Public Service, November 1997, pp. 2, 9.

NEWSPAPER ALLEGIANCES

It was clear throughout the post-war period that newspapers had political allegiances and that these coloured how they covered news generally and political news in particular (see, for example, Cmd 7700, June 1949, Appendix VII). But since newspapers were unregulated and were private property, it was not possible to legislate against such practices. The problem was that there was a lack of diversity and the balance of political preferences always favoured the Conservative Party. This was most evident during elections. In 1997, however, there was a significant change in newspaper allegiances (see table below). *The Sun* backed the Labour Party and, at one point, there was a possibility that the traditionally Conservative *Daily Mail* would also follow suit (see English, 1995). Many, though, were concerned that the price for the support of *The Sun* was an absence of media cross-ownership legislation which might impact on Murdoch's News International.

Daily newspaper partisanship and circulation, general elections in 1979, 1983, 1992 and 1997 (circulation in '000s)

	1979	1983	1992	1997
Daily Express	2,458 Cons.	1,936 Cons.	1,525 Cons.	1,220 Cons.
The Sun	3,942 Cons.	4,155 Cons.	3,571 Cons.	3,842 Lab.
Daily Mail	1,973 Cons.	1,834 Cons.	1,675 Cons.	2,151 Cons.
Daily Mirror	3,783 Lab.	3,267 Lab.	2,903 Lab.	3,084 Lab.
Daily Telegraph	1,358 Cons.	1,284 Cons.	1,038 Cons.	1,134 Cons.
The Guardian	275 Lab.	417 not Cons. landslide	429 Lab. victory, more Lib. Dems	401 Lab.
The Times	not published	321 Cons.	386 Cons.	719 Eurosceptic
Financial Times			290 not Cons. victory	307 Lab.
The Independent			390 no endorsement	251 Lab.
Today			533 Cons.	
Daily Star	880 neutral	1,313 Cons.	806 Cons.	648 Lab.
Total circulation	14,669	14,527	13,546	13,757
Total Cons. circulation	9,731 (66%)	10,843 (75%)	9,534 (70%)	4,505 (33%)
Total Lab. circulation	4,058 (28%)	3,267 (22%)	3,332 (25%)	8,533 (62%)

Sources: Figures derived from I. Crewe and M. Harrop, *Political Communications: The British General Election of 1983*, Cambridge: Cambridge University Press, 1986, p. 139; C. Seymour-Ure, 'Editorial opinion in the national press', *Parliamentary Affairs* 50(4), 1966, pp. 586–608, p. 591.

References

Benn, T. (1987) *Out of the Wilderness: Diaries 1963–67*, London: Hutchinson.

Briggs, A. (1995) *Competition: The History of Broadcasting in the United Kingdom*, Oxford: Oxford University Press.

Brittan, S. (1987) 'The fight for freedom in broadcasting', *Political Quarterly* 58(1), pp. 3–24.

Curtis, L. (1984) *Ireland and the Propaganda War*, London: Pluto Press.

Dahl, H. F. (1994) 'The pursuit of media history', *Media, Culture and Society* 16(4), pp. 551–64.

Day, R. (1989) *Grand Inquisitor*, London: Pan Books.

English, D. (1995) 'Tony at our table', *The Guardian*, 6 October 1995, p. 19.

Evans, H. (1984) *Good Times, Bad Times*, London: Coronet.

Harris, R. (1991) *Good and Faithful Servant*, London: Faber and Faber.

McCarthy, Lord (1983) *The Feasibility of Establishing a New Labour Newspaper*, Report to the TUC, London.

Maddox, B. (1972) *Beyond Babel: New Directions in Communications*, London: Andre Deutsch.

Melvern, L. (1986) *The End of the Street*, London: Methuen.

Negrine, R. (1982) 'The press and the Suez crisis: a myth re-examined', *Historical Journal* 25(4), pp. 975–83.

Negrine, R. (1988) *Satellite Television*, London: Routledge.

Negrine, R. (1994) *Politics and the Mass Media in Britain*, London: Routledge.

Norton-Taylor, R. (1994) 'BBC connived with MI6 to oust Nasser', *The Guardian*, 16 September 1994, p. 8.

Potter, J. (1989) *Independent Television in Britain. Volume 3 Politics and Control, 1968–1980*, London: Macmillan.

Seymour-Ure, C. (1974) *The Political Impact of Mass Media*, London: Constable.

Shaw, T. (1996) *Eden, Suez and the Mass Media*, London: I. B. Taurus.

Snoddy, R. (1993) *The Good, the Bad and the Unacceptable*, London: Faber and Faber.

Somerfield, S. (1979) *Banner Headlines*, Sussex: Scan Books.

Taylor, A. J. P. (1974) *Beaverbrook*, London: Penguin.

Tunstall, J. (1980) 'Research for the Royal Commission on the Press, 1974–7', in M. Bulmer, ed., *Social Research and Royal Commissions*, London: George Allen & Unwin, pp. 122–49.

Tunstall, J. (1983) *The Media in Britain*, London: Constable.

Wilson, H. (1961) *Pressure Group: The Campaign for Commercial Television*, London: Secker & Warburg.

Guide to further reading

General

There is a plethora of books on the mass media. The list included in this section provides general overviews on the topics dealt with in this volume. All are accessible in style and content.

Boyd-Barrett, O., Seymour-Ure, C. and Tunstall, J., *Studies on the Press*, London: HMSO, 1977.

Curran, J. and Seaton, J., *Power Without Responsibilty*, 5th edn, London: Routledge, 1997.

Franklin, B., *Newszak and News Media*, London: Edward Arnold, 1997.

Franklin, B., *Packaging Politics*, London: Edward Arnold, 1994.

Negrine, R., *Politics and the Mass Media in Britain*, 2nd edn, London: Routledge, 1994.

Seymour-Ure, C., *Political Impact of Mass Media*, London: Constable, 1974.

Seymour-Ure, C., *The Press and Broadcasting in Britain since 1945*, 2nd edn, Oxford: Blackwell, 1995.

Television

The development of the broadcasting system is covered in many of the books listed in the above section. However, more extensive treatment of the historical documents cane be found in Anthony Smith's *British Broadcasting*, London: David and Charles, 1974. The history of the BBC is covered in Asa Briggs's five volumes on *The History of Broadcasting in the United Kingdom*, Oxford University Press. The five volumes are: Volume I *The Birth of Broadcasting*, 1961; Volume II *The Golden Age of Wireless*, 1965; Volume III *The War of Words*, 1970; Volume IV *Sound and Vision*, 1979; Volume V *Competition*, 1995.

On commercial television, the history is covered in B. Sendall's *Independent Television in Britain*: Volume I *Origin and Foundation 1946–1962*, 1983, and Volume II *Expansion and Change, 1958–1968*, 1983. Two later volumes, by Jeremy Potter, complete the account. These are: Volume III *Politics and Expansion, 1968–1980*, 1989, and Volume IV *Companies and Progress, 1968–1980*, 1990. All published by Macmillan. A general account of broadcasting history is also provided by Andrew Crissell in his *An Introductory History to Broadcasting*, London: Routledge, 1997.

More general accounts of broadcasting issues can be found in the following:

Atkinson, D. and Raboy, M. (eds), *Public Service Broadcasting: The Challenges of the Twenty-first Century*, Paris: Unesco, 1997.
Barnett, S. and Curry, A., *The Battle for the BBC: A British Conspiracy?* London: Aurum Press, 1994.
Collins, R., Locksley, G. and Garnham, N., *The Economics of Television*, London: Sage, 1988.
Docherty, D., Morrison, D. and Tracey, M., *Keeping Faith? Channel Four and its Audience*, Luton: John Libbey, 1988.
Graham, A. and Davies, G., *Broadcasting, Society and Policy in the Multimedia Age*, Luton: John Libbey, 1997.
Hoggart, R. and Morgan, J. (eds), *The Future of Broadcasting*, London: Macmillan, 1982.
Hood, S. (ed.), *Behind the Scenes: The Structure of British Television in the Nineties*, London: Lawrence and Wishart, 1994.
McDonnell, J. (ed.), *Public Service Broadcasting*, London: Routledge, 1991.

'New media'

Often material in this field has a tendency towards prediction. The following volumes give overviews of the many issues pertaining to old and new media and the relations between the two. Kenneth

Dyson and Peter Humphreys have edited two volumes on these topics: *Broadcasting and New Media Policies in Western Europe*, London: Routledge, 1988, and *The Political Economy of Communications*, London: Routledge, 1991. Both also include material on individual European countries.

Two earlier volumes, by Ralph Negrine, trace some of the histories: *Cable Television and the Future of Broadcasting*, London: Routledge, 1985, and *Satellite Television*, London: Routledge, 1988.

Finally, a contemporary overview of telecommunications and other media can be found in Richard Collins and Christina Murroni's *New Media, New Policies,* Cambridge: Polity, 1996.

Television and politics

Writings on 'television and politics' tend to focus on specific areas or topics. Overviews on broadcasting and the political system can be found in Asa Briggs's *Governing the BBC*, London: BBC, 1979, and in Tom Burns's *The BBC: Public Institution and Private World*, London: Macmillan, 1977. Also useful are Michael Tracey's *The Production of Political Television*, London: Routledge and Kegan Paul, 1978, and Philip Schlesinger's *Putting 'Reality' Together,* London: Routledge, 1978. One overview which gives detailed accounts of the coverage of elections on television is Jay Blumler and Michael Gurevitch's *The Crisis of Public Communication*, London: Routledge, 1995.

The televising of Parliament

Two texts on this topic cover a great deal of the relevant material. J. Blumler, B. Franklin, D. Mercer and B. Tutt, *Monitoring the Public Experiment in Televising the Proceedings of the House of Commons*, published as the First Report from the Select Committee on the Televising of Proceedings of the House, Session 1989–90, Vol. 1, HC 265-I, London: HMSO, 1990, provides a full account of the debates and the initial television coverage of the House. Bob Franklin's *Televising Democracies*, London: Routledge, 1992, provides a similarly useful account of events in Britain and overseas.

Guide to further reading

The press

As with broadcasting, Anthony Smith covers the development of the press up to 1974 in his *The British Press since the War*, London: David and Charles, 1974. Other historical overviews can be found in G. Boyce, J. Curran and P. Wingate (eds), *Newspaper History: From the 17th Century to the Present*, London: Constable, 1978. A history of the early years of the press can be found in Alan Lee's *The Origins of the Popular Press 1855–1914*, London: Croom Helm, 1976, whilst a political history can be found in Stephen Koss's *The Rise and Fall of the Political Press in Britain*, London: Fontana, 1990.

Well-informed accounts of the industry and issues relating to it can be found in J. Tunstall, *Newspaper Power: The New National Press in Britain*, Oxford: Oxford University Press, 1995.

J. Tunstall and M. Palmer's *Media Moguls*, London: Routledge, 1991, focuses on proprietors. There is, in fact, a considerable library on publishers. These would include Tom Bower, *Maxwell the Outsider*, London: Mandarin, 1991, and L. Chester and J. Fenby, *The Fall of the House of Beaverbrook*, London: Andre Deutsch, 1979, amongst many.

Finally, one book which looks at changing newspaper agendas and the risk of 'tabloidisation' is Matthew Engel's *Tickle the Public*, London: Gollancz, 1996.

The press and politics

A good account of the relationship between the press and Parliament, and more generally the press and politics, is Colin Seymour-Ure's 'Parliament and mass communication in the twentieth century', in S. Walkland (ed.), *The House of Commons in the Twentieth Century*, Oxford: Clarendon Press, 1979.

Accounts about the Lobby system and Lobby practices are provided in James Margach's *The Abuse of Power*, London: W. H. Allen, 1978, and *The Anatomy of Power*, London: W. H. Allen, 1979. Michael Cockerell's work on this is also well known. *Sources Close to the Prime Minister*, by M. Cockerel, P. Hennessey and D. Walker, London: Macmillan, 1984, covers the period up to the mid-1980s. Nic Jones's *Soundbites and Spin Doctors*, London: Indigo, 1996, brings the account up to date.

Finally, a useful guide to HMSO publications is the *Index to Official Publications CD-ROM* from Chadwyck-Healey. This lists all publications from 1980 onwards and so provides an easy route to finding out what is available about the media (and other topics).

Index